THE EPIC VOYAGES OF MAUD BERRIDGE

The seafaring diaries of a Victorian lady

Sally Berridge

BLOOMSBURY

LONDON · OXFORD · NEW YORK · NEW DELHI · SYDNEY

Adlard Coles Nautical
An imprint of Bloomsbury Publishing Plc

50 Bedford Square
London
WC1B 3DP
UK

1385 Broadway
New York
NY 10018
USA

www.bloomsbury.com
www.adlardcoles.com

Adlard Coles is a trademark of Bloomsbury Publishing Plc

First published 2018

British Library Cataloguing-in-Publication Data
A catalogue record for this book is available from the British Library.

Library of Congress Cataloguing-in-Publication data has been applied for.

ISBN: HB: 978-1-4729-5423-7
TPB: 978-1-4729-5662-0
ePDF: 978-1-4729-5420-6
ePub: 978-1-4729-5422-0

2 4 6 8 10 9 7 5 3 1

Typeset by Deanta Global Publishing Services, Chennai, India
Printed and bound in Great Britain by CPI Group (UK) Ltd,
Croydon, CRO 4YY

Bloomsbury Publishing Plc makes every effort to ensure that the papers
used in the manufacture of our books are natural, recyclable products made
from wood grown in well-managed forests. Our manufacturing processes
conform to the environmental regulations of the country of origin.

To find out more about our authors and books visit www.bloomsbury.com.

To Maud Berridge, truly one of Britannia's daughters.

Acknowledgements

Dr Ian Petrie of the University of Pennsylvania has been of invaluable help to me. He came across my family tree on the internet when he was researching the log of the *Clarence*, an East Indiaman; Henry Berridge had been first mate on board at the time and Ian was investigating the crew. When he heard I was writing about Maud Berridge, he pointed me towards important books and papers that would assist me in putting her story together as well as finding historical information for me from both the National Maritime Museum at Greenwich and the Maritime Museum at St John's, Newfoundland. I am completely indebted to him.

Audrey Russell of Melbourne very kindly scanned and sent me several photos of Maud and Henry from her Timperley archives.

I also appreciate the assistance of the West Australian Police History Society Inc and their generosity in letting me use the photo of a young WH Timperley.

The Little Baddow Historical Society kindly sent me biographical details of Jesse Berridge.

I want to thank Fiona and Simon Luckhurst for reading the manuscript and making useful and pertinent comments.

Contents

A Note to Maud

My Dear Great-Grandmother Maud

I wonder what you would think of your diaries being published. From the way they were written I do believe that they were intended for the eyes of your sons Harold and Jesse, your 'darling boys', when they were old enough to appreciate them, and perhaps your brothers and their families as well. Some 134 years have passed since you wrote them: your sons and grandsons are dead now, but your strength as an unsung Victorian woman still shines through your words. I hope that I am keeping a torch lit for you, as your descendant and your admirer.

You died 30 years before I was born, so when I found your diaries on the website of the National Maritime Museum at Greenwich in London in the course of family research, I was very excited. I had heard of your husband Henry (Harry as you called him), a master mariner, but I wanted to know more about you.

Your diaries showed me a woman of substance: you never complained about the bad weather or uncomfortable conditions on board, or about seasickness. You made interesting comments about others. You were always loyal to your Harry. You showed a keen interest in other cultures. You endured the boredom of the calm times and the danger of the rough ones with equal stoicism. Your faith was always strong for you.

I suppose you were a loving and dutiful wife in the Victorian ideal, but I think that you weren't subservient to

Harry. It seems that you truly admired him and his skilled seamanship. I love it that he took you tea in bed or read you poetry on deck by the light of the new moon. I like to think that the two of you had a genuine love match. As happens so often, even now, it is the men who live in the limelight, while the wives are in the shadows. Yet I ask, would Henry have been such a good captain if you had not travelled with him?

In 2016, I was on a cruise ship north of Sydney that made a temporary, watery disturbance in the sea, leaving no trace of its passage. In 1883, the sailing ship *Superb* had made her way up this very coast, and at some point I crossed paths with the watery disturbance you and Henry had made when you set off from Newcastle, New South Wales, to turn east across the Pacific Ocean towards San Francisco. A fragile connection, but one that has grown to feel more secure as I have investigated your story.

I feel so privileged to have come to know you just a bit, and to share some of your story. Joanna Trollope wrote *Britannia's Daughters: Women of the British Empire* about 100 years after your voyages. As she puts it, many delicately nurtured but clever young Victorian women were 'imprisoned in the unbearable emptiness of respectable drawing rooms, like dolls waiting for men to come in and wind them up to a brief animation before leaving the room again and abandoning them to desperate monotony.'[1] You managed to escape this fate, through the chance for freedom and a degree of self-expression presented by your marriage to a sea captain. It seems as though seasickness, the cramped conditions and dangers on board were a small price for you to pay.

I wish I had known you.

Your loving great-granddaughter
Sally

Introduction

'As Henry says, we have only one life to live, and he cannot be at home, and it is very hard for us to be separated so much, and a very unpleasant way of spending our lives when one is thousands of miles away.'[1]

My great-grandmother Maud Berridge (née Timperley) was the wife of Henry Berridge, master mariner and captain of three three-masted sailing ships: *Walmer Castle* (built in 1836), *Highflyer* (built in 1861) and *Superb*[2] (built in 1866), all owned by Greens at Blackwall Yard, London. Henry sailed these ships many times from London to Melbourne, taking migrants to Australia. Maud accompanied him on five of these voyages, travelling on the *Walmer Castle* once (1869–1870) and on the *Superb* four times (1880–1881, 1882–1883, 1883–1884, 1886–1887) to Australia and back to England (and, in 1883–1884, from Melbourne to San Francisco before returning to England).

Maud may have written more diaries of her voyages, but only two remain: a fragment from 1880–1881 and a full account from 1883–1884. These are the core material of this book. They were deposited with the National Maritime Museum at Greenwich, London by her son Jesse in 1948. The 1880 fragment has no cover, and the 1883–1884 account is written in pen and ink in two volumes. The first is a blue leather-covered book about 15cm (6in) square, and the second is a larger dark red leather-covered notebook about 24cm (9½ in) square. The binding of both is battered and the

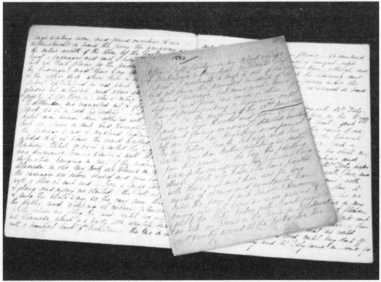

Maud's diaries of her 1883–84 travels.

pages have yellowed. They are now digitised and are therefore accessible via the internet.

I have been unable to find details about Maud's other three voyages apart from shipping records in Melbourne so I have used material written by others that describes life on board: a diary (1869–1870), the *Superb Gazette* of 1882 and a letter (1886–1887), all incidentally giving masculine views of life on board for these voyages.

In 1869, as a new bride, Maud sailed on her first voyage to Melbourne via the Cape of Good Hope and back to London via Cape Horn on the *Walmer Castle*. Henry was taking the wheel for the first time as captain. Then there is a gap of about 11 years, presumably for child–rearing. In 1880 she wrote a diary of her voyage to Melbourne with her two sons, Jesse aged six and Harold aged eight, on board the *Superb*. Only part of this diary remains. I remember my grandfather, Harold, telling me he went on a sailing ship as a child and had to tap the weevils out of the ship's biscuits before he could eat them.

Maud's extensive 1883–1884 diaries cover her travels with Captain Henry in the *Superb* from London: first travelling south to catch the Roaring Forties – strong winds south of the Cape of Good Hope, which also bring enormous waves, storms and icebergs – and then east to Melbourne. After a short stay it was on to Newcastle, NSW to pick up a load of coal (and visit Sydney), from there sailing across the Pacific to San Francisco to unload the coal. After having spent two months there they picked up a load of wheat, and sailed down the west coast of the Americas, round Cape Horn, and on to (then) Cooktown, County Cork, Ireland to unload the wheat. Their return to England from San Francisco took about five months (no Panama Canal then), and the whole voyage some 14 months. She describes Melbourne, Newcastle, Sydney and San Francisco in 1883 as well as their travels to see the geysers in Sonoma County.

The diaries give a woman's perspective of life on a sailing ship. She does occasionally mention some other wives who travelled with their captain husbands, so perhaps it wasn't uncommon for these women to travel in this way, but seemingly it wasn't written about much, or else the diaries have faded from view. Her diaries are substantial and well written; clearly she had had a good education and was proficient in grammar and spelling. In addition, she managed a pen and ink at sea.

Maud describes her role on the ship indirectly. For instance, she mentions 'working', which turns out to be various knitting and sewing projects. In addition, she is active in the concerts (including a short opera), dances and on-deck competitions such as quoits, which the passengers used as a means of whiling away the long and sometimes uncomfortable journeys; she organises church services for Sundays and plays the piano for hymns and for Henry to sing at concerts, and occasionally sings herself; and she oversees raffles and other activities that make contributions to various seamen's charities. Moreover, she looks after passengers who are unwell, and she herself suffers badly from seasickness.

Maud's diaries omit the everyday truths that are self-evident to the writer, such as her family background and the mechanics of life on board ship. Cultural norms, too, are taken for granted. So, in order to flesh out the backstory, in the first part of this book I have summarised some of Maud and Henry's family history and given some detail of life aboard a sailing ship. I have also looked briefly at women in Victorian times and their interest in writing diaries, as well as at the importance of the Merchant Navy to Britain at that time, and migration to Australia. In addition, I have provided some of the history of Greens of Blackwall, Henry's employers and owner of the ships he captained, along with some details of the ships, especially the *Superb*.

In the process of creating context I looked at passenger lists, shipping records, crew agreements and any other relevant material I could find to add detail to what Maud wrote. The internet has been a deep source of historical material – from family information via the regular censuses and birth, marriage and death records, to old photos and other more general contextual material.

MAUD AND HENRY – FAMILY BACKGROUND

Maud was the daughter of William Postles Timperley and Elizabeth Bradney Evans, and was born in Shrewsbury, Shropshire on 3 November 1845. Her father was a clerk in holy orders; her mother was a goddaughter of the prime minister, Sir Robert Peel, who was apparently very good to her. Maud had three older brothers: William Henry, Francis (Frank) and Oughton.

William Postles Timperley is believed to be a descendant of a famous family of Timperley landed gentry, connected to the Duke of Norfolk, who were distant cousins of Anne Boleyn. They purchased Hintlesham Hall in Suffolk in 1454, but, later, family mythology has it that some less-than-astute political allegiances saw them lose both this residence and their high position. However, the line has continued and there are currently Timperleys and their descendants in England, America and Australia.

The 1851 census has Maud living in Warwick with her mother as head of the household, since her father and two older brothers had gone to seek their fortunes in Western Australia.[3] No records are apparent for the 1861 census, but Maud Timperley was married in Warwick St Mary on 26 August 1869 to my great-grandfather, Captain Henry Berridge (1837–1891), and he had obtained his Master Mariner's certification (i.e. he was certified to captain a ship) in 1866.[4] (See Appendix I.)

Henry Berridge was the third-oldest of 12 children. His father was Robert Sheppard Berridge, a surgeon (1802–1851), and his mother was Elizabeth Howcutt (1812–1873) of Leicester. He was born on 12 December 1837 in Melton Mowbray, Leicestershire.

The 1851 census (30 March) has Henry living at home with his family, including a six-week-old sister. His father died just a few months later, on 19 September, when Henry was 14. The family must have been quite well off, as demonstrated by the presence of Henry's baby photos, and supported by the fact that the 1851 census details staff: a nursemaid, a governess, a cook, a housemaid and a stable boy. Despite this affluent background, in the January of 1852 – following the death of his father – 15-year-old Henry took to the sea, starting his career in the Merchant Navy as a midshipman (middy) on the ship *Success* travelling from London to Melbourne. When the ship was sold in Melbourne he worked his passage back to England on the *Lochnagar* as an ordinary seaman later that year.

Henry then worked as a midshipman on the *Owen Glendower*, Greens Blackwall Line,[5] between 18 July 1853 and 25 May 1856. This ship was an Indiaman built by Greens in London in 1839 (852 tons), and was registered to travel between London and Madras.[6]

The table in Appendix II details Henry's statement of service in the Merchant Navy from 1852 to 1866 when he was certified as a master mariner. Once he joined the *Owen Glendower*, he stayed with Greens Blackwallers for the rest of his career, climbing the mates' ladder until he became first mate on the *Clarence*, then captaining the *Walmer Castle*, the *Highflyer* and the *Superb*, so Greens must have had confidence in his skills.

Henry had been on sailing ships for some 34 years by his last voyage, with about 14 of these spent captaining ships to Melbourne and back to England. An on-board newspaper, the *Superb Hemisphere* (1888), describes the *Superb* returning to London via Cape Town, although the writer does not specify whether Henry was the captain.

Part 1 of the book, in describing the background to Maud's diaries, gives some information on the world of sailing ships, on Greens of Blackwall, and on three of their ships. Life on board and the way in which sailing ships functioned are also explored, as are ideas concerning women on board, and there are some indirect descriptions of three of Maud's voyages.

Maud's diaries (unabridged) form the second part of the book and speak for themselves, while Part 3 consists of afternotes: how and when Maud and Henry died, how their sons grew up, what happened to the *Superb*, and the end of the Age of Sail. The book finishes with some family traces and reflections.

PART 1

Background to Maud's diaries

I

Nineteenth-century sailing ships

Throughout the 19th century, the sea and ships were the lifeblood of Britain for commerce, exploration and defence. The East India Company was originally set up during Elizabethan times to trade with the East Indies, but it found richer pickings in India during the 16th–19th centuries, with the result that Britain eventually dominated half the world's trade in cotton, silk, indigo, saltpetre, tea and opium. At the height of this trade, Britain registered about 40 per cent of the world's merchant ships; in some years of the mid-19th century, for instance, four new ships a day were completed to add to the merchant service.[1]

There were three main sailing institutions and groups of sailors in Britain: the Royal Navy, the Merchant Service and the free-traders (including Isaac Gulliver from Dorset, a very successful smuggler and my four-times great-grandfather[2]). The Merchant Service was not a single organisation, but a collective of owners and crews. It was vital for Britain's economy, being key to the nation's position as the centre of world trade; in 1899, for example, the Merchant Service comprised 10,998 ships, dwarfing the tally for the next-largest service, that of the USA, which had a mere 2,739 ships. In 1826 there were 160,000 seagoing crewmen in the Merchant Service, compared with 21,000 in the Navy.[3]

GREENS OF BLACKWALL

In the 17th century the King's ships were built at docks at Blackwall on the Thames, and it was here that the East Indiamen were purpose-developed for trade with India; the East India Company became innovative in ship design as part of its high standards and efficiency.

In the 18th century the Merchant Service had more freedom in the design and construction of its ships than the Navy. This was because the latter was at one point riddled with dishonesty and subsequently had to develop and administer severe rules in an attempt to curb such self-interest, rules that stifled innovation in ship design.

The Napoleonic Wars of 1802–1813 saw many troops embarking from the Blackwall Yard and the Brunswick Docks. Around this time, George Green, son of a Chelsea brewer, was a 15-year-old apprentice in the Blackwall Yard, and through hard work (and marrying the boss's daughter) eventually became a partner in the ship-building enterprise. After the death of his father-in-law in 1810, Green took on a new partner, Sir Robert Wigram. Nine years later, Wigram retired and sold his share of the business to George Green (half share), and to his sons Money and Henry Loftus Wigram (a quarter share each), for £40,500. He died in 1830, and the company continued as Green and Wigram until the partnership expired in 1843. At this point, the families divided the shipyard between them, with Richard Green taking over the eastern portion of the yard, and Money Wigram the western portion.

Dicky, the son of George Green, had a reputation as an excellent shipowner: he designed his ships for comfort for officers, men and passengers, and they were well built and well maintained. He died in 1863, having been revered the world over. He was a charitable man, generous to the surrounding community, and he and his father established a Sailor's Home, the Trinity Schools, and the Trinity Chapel and alms houses in Poplar. He was staunchly conservative in his ideas about ship building and loved teak and oak: it was only after his death that iron Blackwallers were built: the *Superb*, the *Carlisle Castle* and the *Melbourne*.[4]

Design of the Blackwall frigates

Lubbock describes Blackwall ships as bluff-bowed and apple-cheeked in design, with little dead rise in the mid sections and long poops. This shape meant that fewer seas were shipped over the fo'c'sle head. The short main decks were used for stowing the longboat, as well as being the site of the pigpens, chicken coops and cow stalls. In addition, the first- and second-class galleys were here.

The placement of the tiller was as it had been since Elizabethan times, on the lower deck, and the wheel was forward of the mizzen mast. The ships, as well as the deck and cabin fittings, were finely made of English oak and Malabar teak, hard woods that resisted hard seas.[5]

Basil Lubbock writes:

> They were conservative ships, and prided themselves on their weatherliness ... Carrying away spars and even sails was considered bad seamanship on a Blackwaller, where everything was of the best and no doubt the reason for their singular freedom from accidents ... Seaworthiness was *sine qua non* in a first class passenger ship. Beautifully kept, regularly overhauled, every beam and plank of picked wood, every rope-yarn strong enough to hang a man, and every sail without a patch ... Accidents were few and far between ... No Blackwaller ever had to shorten sail to prevent straining in a heavy sea... they were as lively, dry and buoyant as corks.[6]

It is easy to understand why a young Henry Berridge would have sought a position on a Greens East Indiaman, and he duly signed on as a midshipman on The *Owen Glendower*, bound for Bombay, when he was about 19. He worked his way through the ranks, and on the *Clarence*, became first mate on 15 May 1859, when he was about 25, and stayed with the ship for seven years, becoming first mate on 15 May 1861. He gained his Master's Certificate on 13 July 1866, and stayed with Greens for the rest of his career as a master mariner. His first recorded voyage as captain was the one in 1870 on the *Walmer Castle* to Melbourne with his bride Maud. He then sailed the *Highflyer* to Melbourne and back five times (all without Maud), and sailed the *Superb* to Melbourne and back at least seven times, with Maud accompanying him four times.[7]

The Walmer Castle
Greens' *Walmer Castle* was a wooden clipper built in 1855 by W Pile, Sunderland, for the Blackwall Line. She was 1,064 tons, 192ft long, 35ft broad and 22ft deep. After making two voyages to Melbourne, she was transferred in 1858 to the Madras, Calcutta and China trade, in which she spent ten years. In 1869, she again sailed to Melbourne with Henry as captain, for Maud's first voyage. After this the ship went back to the India trade and in 1874 she was sold to J and K Welch and converted to a barque rig that plied between England, China, India and Australia. In 1877 she was destroyed by fire while loading at Samarang.[8]

The Highflyer
The *Highflyer* was purpose built for the London–Australia run in 1861.[9] She was 1,111 tons, but no statistics are available for her length, depth and breadth. As with the rest of the Blackwall Line, she was well appointed, as attested by an advertisement in the British *Standard* newspaper (19 May 1874), which notes: 'Messrs. Greens' ship *Highflyer* will leave the East India Docks on 25th May bound for Melbourne, Port Philip Bay. It has very superior accommodation for first, second and third class passengers; the saloon is furnished, and the ship will carry a surgeon.'

The Superb

Superb is a common ship's name. Henry's Superb (official number 54755) was the first iron ship to be built by Greens at the Blackwall shipyard on the edge of the Thames, more or less opposite what is now the National Maritime Museum at Greenwich in London. The use of iron was innovative at the time, and it was used because of its greater strength and powers of resistance compared with wood. Moreover, wooden ships were more susceptible to fire than iron ships and had many working parts that needed to be secured or that could come loose in a storm.[10]

The Superb was launched in 1866 and became a favourite passenger ship to Melbourne. Her statistics were: 1,451 tons, 230.3ft in length, poop 77ft and fo'c'sle 45ft. According to Lubbock, the Superb had several fine passages to her credit when commanded by Captain Berridge: 1881 – 76 days; 1886 – 74 days; 1879 – 78 days.[11]

TRAVELLING TO AND FROM AUSTRALIA
IN THE 1800S

The discovery of immense goldfields in Australia and the subsequent gold rushes meant that Londoners wanted first- and second-class berths as passengers. Blackwall designers took this into account, and produced the only British ships purpose-fitted in this way to meet the demands of more selective clientele.[12]

Ships usually left London in late autumn, sailing south around the Cape of Good Hope and arriving in Australia for the Australian summer. Sam Jefferson's book Clipper Ships and the Golden Age of Sail shows a contemporary map of the principal trade routes of sailing ships during this time, including the Great Eastern Route.[13]

The journey from England to Australia took about two and a half to three months, depending on the ship, the weather and the skill of the captain. Although the Suez Canal had been completed on 17 November 1869 it was not navigable by a sailing ship unless a costly tug was employed for the length of the canal. Henry's voyages to Melbourne therefore took an alternative route, well known to him, possibly the Great Eastern Route shown on Jefferson's map: southwards down the west coast of Africa and around the Cape of Good Hope, travelling 40° to 50° south (Maud shows these latitudes in her 1883 diary) to catch the Roaring Forties. Then it was north-east towards Cape Otway, along the southern coast of Western Australia and Victoria, and across the Australian Bight before reaching Melbourne. This part of the southern coast of Australia was extremely dangerous; shipwrecks were common.

The ship would be re-stocked with supplies and cargo when in port, then instead of turning around, had to continue east to take advantage of the south-easterly Trade winds. This meant travelling far enough south to pick up the winds, so icebergs were a common hazard on the cold and extremely windy trip around the notorious Cape Horn if returning that way. Once around the Horn, it was a turn northwards across the Equator again, through the Doldrums and towards Europe to catch the north-east Trade winds. The *Superb* often went to Queenstown (now Cobh) in County Cork, Ireland, presumably to unload cargo on the return voyage before she continued to London.

In the mid-1800s, Henry's voyages were part of the great immigration schemes of Britain and Australia. Industrialisation in Britain had brought crowds to the cities, where there was consequently rank overcrowding, poverty and disease. The British government wanted to reduce this urban population, and at the same time address the shortage of various kinds of agricultural labourers and domestic servants in Australia. Suitable young, healthy and useful or skilled people were therefore given assisted passages by the British government, with the funds often coming from the sale of land. These emigrants were paid between £2 and £6 per person to cover the entire cost of the journey – financial assistance that offset both the fact that it was more expensive to travel to Australia than to Canada or the USA, and, the fact that Australia was deemed by many to be a less attractive destination. Numerous unassisted migrants also sailed to Australia. Such people were often wealthy merchants looking for opportunities in the growing economy of the colony, and many others travelled to seek their fortunes on the goldfields.

Life on board a Victorian sailing ship
The myth of the romantic beauty of the sailing ship in full flight is a common one, but in reality it was just that: a myth, one that masked the dangers, trials, tribulations and discom forts that the voyage would inevitably bring. This was particularly true for the steerage (third-class) passengers, who had to sleep in crowded, smelly spaces between decks, in bunks or hammocks, and with single men and women segregated and different rules for each group.

Second-class passengers fared a little better than steerage ones, having small cabins, while first-class or saloon passengers such as Maud were in larger private cabins that were fitted out relatively comfortably with their own beds, linen and furniture that had been brought on board at the start of the voyage. According to Dorothy and James Volo, the captain's cabin would have had a skylight that provided light and ventilation in good weather, and there would have been furniture such as a sofa, maybe a small stove, and a sea chest. Perhaps navigational aids might have cluttered the captain's table.[14] Maud mentions her birds very briefly (presumably caged birds such as canaries), and she brought her dear dog Boxer with her as well. The marital bed may have been mounted on gimbals to provide some stability in rough seas (Maud mentions the bed swaying).[15]

Because there was feed on board for the chickens, sheep, pigs and goats (and possibly also cows and horses), rats, weevils and cockroaches were rife; many passengers of all classes found their dogs and cats very useful in trying to contain vermin numbers. Maud herself describes an occasion as they are nearing home from Los Angeles and have a cargo of wheat on board when they try to clear out the rats from between decks. Her dog Boxer was an enthusiastic ratter.

Moreover, whatever their accommodation, all classes had to deal with the conditions meted out to them by the ship and by the prevailing weather: seasickness; poor ventilation, especially in heavy seas or rain when the ports and dead-lights[16] were closed; poor food for most of the passengers, especially towards the end of a long voyage; the possibility of illness or disease; few recreational opportunities for most passengers; and extreme changes in temperature and climate. Heavy seas could enter the portholes or wash over the decks and enter the living spaces of all to flood their possessions, including the mattresses they slept on.

There was real danger, too: extreme weather that could lead to a shipwreck; mistakes in navigation; fire – lighting was with candles, and there were cooking fires in the galley; the loss of sails or masts in storms; even the possibility of collisions with other ships in fog. For the crew up aloft there was an additional danger, that of falling from the rigging – Maud mentions one fall, as does Thomas Miller, both fortunately resulting in injuries less serious than might be expected. The voyage was thus a mixture of boredom when the weather was calm, alternating with high winds and seas that generally brought rather too much excitement.

One must remember, too, that there was nowhere to get off if passengers decided they had had enough; they were in it for the long haul, and this fact alone could cause depression and anxiety and tax the mettle of even those of the steadiest nature. Maud describes the sad plight of one Mr Andrews, who succumbs to depression, as well as saying several times that a sea voyage reveals a person's true nature.

Food and water
For a non-stop voyage from London to Australia of largely unknown duration, and with no refrigeration, it was imperative for the ship to be self-sufficient in water and both

fresh and preserved foods, with enough spare to allow for delays, such as unexpectedly calm weather. On some ships, fresh water was brought on board in barrels and an allowance eked out to passengers and crew for the duration of the voyage. To supplement this, rainwater would be collected in sails set out on deck. Sometimes, as we know from Thomas Miller's account, there was a condensing engine[17] (and engineer) on board, as was the case on the *Superb*, to provide a reliable source of fresh water from seawater.

The captain was the person ultimately responsible for ensuring that a ship was adequately provisioned, as is attested by the statement at the top of the 1869 passenger list for the *Walmer Castle*: 'I hereby certify that the provisions actually laden on board this ship are sufficient according to the requirements of the Passenger's Act, for 30 Statute Adults for a voyage of 140 days.' The Passenger's Act had come about because in earlier times fares had been taken for voyages to Australia with insufficient food and water on board, so many paying passengers had died. So in this case, Henry had signed for 30 passengers despite the fact that there were actually many more, but he had doubled the likely length of the voyage to give a sufficient safety margin for feeding and watering the true number of passengers.

There is no available record of the food supplies taken on board the *Superb* for passengers, but a contemporary list from a ship-store merchant in Liverpool details items put on board a ship to Tasmania that include: tierces (casks slightly larger than barrels) of American beef and suet; barrels of lard; tins of arrowroot, preserved meat, potatoes, soup and bouillon; barrels of flour, sugar, molasses, split peas and oatmeal; firkins (small casks) of butter; hampers of cheese; casks of lime juice, pickles and vinegar; bags of rice, sago, barley and raisins; coffee; salt and pepper; kegs of mustard; and bundles of salt fish.

On top of all of this, there was a crew's agreement for food. For example, for the 52 seamen signed on as crew on the round voyage of the *Superb* from London to Melbourne and back in 1880, there were specified allowances for the crew's food sanctioned by the Board of Trade in 1869. This *Daily Schedule of Victualling for One Man* set out the days of the week and the weekly allowances:

> beef (4 1/2 lbs), flour (1 1/2 lbs), raisins (4 1/2 oz), suet (3 oz), pork (3 3/4 lbs), peas (1 pint), preserved meat (1 1/4 lbs), preserved potatoes 1/4 lbs), tea (1 3/4 oz), coffee (3 1/2 oz), sugar (14 oz), bread (No allowance, no waste), mustard (1 oz per man per week), vinegar (1/2 pint per man per week), lime juice and sugar (As per Act of Parliament).

Some items such as beef were distributed on Sundays, Tuesdays and Fridays. The water allowance was 7 pints (4 litres) per man per day in hot weather and 6 pints (3.4 litres) in cold weather. 'In harbour the allowance was 1 1/2 lbs fresh meat and 1 lb potatoes or yams per day, when procurable. It is understood that the master may substitute one day's provisions for another at his discretion.'[18]

The staple food for seamen was the ship's biscuit, which was:

> notorious for being virtually indestructible and resembling neither biscuit nor bread. Made with flour, a little salt and just enough water to make a stiff dough, sea biscuit was baked into 4x4 inch squares about half an inch thick. Sailors had to soak it to make it edible or nibble around the edges. When the biscuit was poor, it was either too hard or mouldy and wet. It was noted for being filled with weevils and maggots. These pests could be evicted by toasting the cracker or breaking it up into a mug of liquid and skimming off the pests.[19]

As well as these dry and preserved goods for passengers and crew alike, the lifeboats of sailing ships were filled at the start of the voyage with fresh produce such as potatoes and cabbages, and there was also livestock on board: sheep, chickens for meat and eggs, pigs, sometimes goats and dairy cows. Plus, of course, all their fodder. Of necessity there was a butcher on board.

Having been prepared in the galley, meals for those who qualified for them were announced by the boatswain's pipe or whistle: breakfast at 8am, dinner at noon, tea or supper at 5.30pm – a long wait until 8am the next morning for breakfast. However, for some groups of passengers or crew, called 'messes', the unprepared food was instead handed out and they had to make their own arrangements for getting it cooked. This involved semi-commercial interactions with the cook and steward, who were receptive to making deals to ease the life of the passengers – particularly those on the lower decks – trading menial labour such as washing up for some extra coffee or food.[20]

Tools and equipment

In addition to all the food and water, the ship had to carry sufficient suitable materials to enable the crew to carry out running repairs to the ship – not only to the sails and rigging that might blow away in a storm, but also to parts of the ship such as rails that might be damaged by heavy seas. Many ships carried a spare set of sails. Running repairs were carried out on board by a sailmaker and carpenter, who would have stocked up while in port with all the necessary tools, nails, canvas and spare sheets (ropes) of various thicknesses etc, as well as with spare signal flags in case some blew away. Ordinary seamen would mostly carry out the routine tarring of wooden joints and painting, as well as generally tidying the ship before coming into port.

Medical supplies

Injuries and sicknesses of various kinds were also to be expected: occasionally a crew member could fall from the rigging, and crew or passengers could be knocked around in rough seas and break bones. Passengers commonly went to Australia in the hope of improving their health, even though they might have tuberculosis – 'that tell-tale cough' that Maud mentions, which was incurable at that time – and their condition might become worse during the voyage. To treat these people, there was frequently, but not always, a doctor on board with limited medical supplies. And for when medical intervention failed, there would have to be provision for burials at sea; each diary that I have examined has mentioned at least one death.

Navigation: latitudes and longitudes

Key to the safety and success of every voyage at sea is accurate navigation. By the mid-18th century the basics of latitude and longitude were well known: Dava Sobel and William Andrewes in their wonderful book *The Illustrated Longitude: the true story of a genius who solved the greatest scientific problem of his time* describe how early scientists, even those three centuries before Christ, worked out ways in which they and others could describe the location of any place on earth. And thus were developed the ideas of latitude and longitude that even today remain fixed while continents drift and political boundaries change. However, even well into the 18th century, one ship in every seven that left port was never heard from again.[21] By the time of Maud and Henry's voyages, navigation on sailing ships was much more reliable, even though maps and charts could be inaccurate. Experienced sailors like Henry learned from their ship, from the various landfalls on their routes, and from their direction and speed.

Simple navigational aids in Henry's time included the astrolabe, the compass, parallel rulers, a sextant and dividers as well as charts.[22]

LIFE ON BOARD HENRY'S SHIP, THE *SUPERB*

The *Superb* was a Greens Blackwaller, and as such, conditions on board were perhaps better for the seamen than they were on many other ships. As a result, among the crew there was a great deal of pride in the Greens of Blackwall line. The crew normally consisted of the captain, the first, second, third and fourth mates, the boatswain, the midshipmen, the ordinary seamen and some necessary skilled men such as the cooks, butchers, sailmakers, carpenters etc.

Blackwall captains
The most senior member of crew and ultimately responsible for the safekeeping of both the vessel itself and the people aboard, the captain of any ship was an important man and deserved the respect due to a person of rank. 'The captain reigns supreme aboard his ship and his word on all occasions is law.' His duties began 'after the departure of the pilot', after which time he had '… no regular watch but in case of necessity, or should the occasion demand, he will of course be on deck to superintend the work carried on by the officer of the watch … At all times when the captain is not on deck, the command of the ship is entrusted to the officer of the watch who is at liberty to set or take in sail at his own discretion, and is also responsible for the sails being trimmed. It rests on his shoulders to protect the welfare and safety of the ship and those on board. His orders have to be obeyed just as strictly as the captain's.'[23]

It is evident, then, that being a captain of any ship was an important role. Moreover, in order to be a captain of a Blackwaller ship, one had to exhibit truly exceptional seamanship:

Captains of the Blackwall frigates were regarded as having reached the pinnacle of their profession, being paid as much as £5,000 a year and could put 'esquire' after their names ... They were far in advance of the ordinary ship-masters of their day with navigation. They regularly used stars when most navigators were content with a meridian altitude ... Many had an uncanny aptitude for finding fair winds and avoiding calm patches, and many were high-class oceanographers ... They were also naturalists, some took trawl nets or dredges to sea and preserved and classified their specimens ... They were professors of the weather, wise to every doldrum squall, every sudden shift of wind and were expert cyclone dodgers.[24]

These Blackwall captains maintained autocratic, old-fashioned standards of discipline for themselves and all on board, although they were less strict on the Australian run. In return, both shipping companies and passengers valued certain qualities in the captain, including 'extensive nautical experience, the ability to maintain discipline in the ranks of both crew and passengers, and, particularly, the personal warmth so necessary in relating to the wide range of personality types on board'.[25] Presumably Henry exemplified these qualities since he stayed with Greens for so many voyages.

Blackwall officers and crews

Blackwall adopted similarly stringent standards and principles for the hiring and retention of other members of crew aboard their ships, whose number generally amounted to about 64:

> Both in number and quality, the Blackwall frigates surpassed other British merchant ships. The petty officers and men before the mast were carefully selected by the mate aided by the bosun, and submitted to the captain for approval. There was seldom a man aboard who was not an expert rigger, a practical sail maker, a neat marlinspike worker, a burly sail-fister and a good helmsman. For example, in 1875

the *Newcastle* had four mates, a surgeon, 8–11 midshipmen, a bo'sun, carpenter, sail-maker, donkeyman, three quarter-masters, four fore topmen, four main topmen, six forecastle hands, six after-guard, four ordinary seamen, four boys, chief and second steward, about seven other stewards (depending on the number of passengers), two cooks, a butcher and butcher's mate, and a baker and baker's mate.[26]

The company usually opted to choose high-quality men, and a correspondingly high social status was conferred on their officers. This, coupled with the fact that they were known for disciplining their sailors fairly, meant that young noblemen and the sons of professional men regarded it as a privilege to become an officer on board Greens East India Company ships.[27]

First mate
The first mate or first officer had responsibility for virtually everything on board, keeping the morning watch and being on board supervising for most of the day. He would also take command for any manoeuvres, such as tacking, that would require all hands on deck even though the captain might be present to superintend.

Other officers
The second officer kept the middle watch at night and the third officer kept the first watch. Additionally, he could keep watch both day and night and was responsible for navigation. When shortening sail, the third officer went aloft to supervise. The fourth officer kept the middle watch with the second officer and during the day kept the midshipmen gainfully employed or taught them aspects of seamanship.

Midshipmen
Midshipmen's parents paid £60 per voyage for the privilege of providing their sons with an excellent career

opportunity that would lead to them becoming officers and navigators. The parents would also have paid pocket and mess money, and provided a brass-bound uniform (with brass buttons) with cap and badges. Greens' insignia at the time was a white flag bearing a blue rectangle covered by a red cross. The cost of training was lowered for subsequent voyages: £50 for the second; £40 for the third and so on until the 'middy' was promoted to fifth mate, at which stage he had to pay only £1 per month. In addition, there was a charge for their food, which was about £80 per voyage.

On Greens' ships, middies were treated as gentlemen and were provided with plenty of food and rest, and, depending on the captain, they might be invited to dine at his table or be given a glass of spirits at dinnertime. When Henry was a middy he would have had to learn the peculiarities of his ship's etiquette, such as the angle of the cap, whether the brass buttons should be polished, and whether or not he should go barefoot.

Middies had the reputation of being mischievous and possibly lazy, but also of being loyal to their mates and extremely proud of their ships and their role aboard, which generally involved working the mizzen[28] mast, reefing, and furling the sails as required. The lifeboats were also the responsibility of the middies – each was assigned a boat to maintain in good condition to be ready for any emergency. There were also duties on watch and they had to be aloft on the main royal yard ten minutes before sunrise when the horizon was at its most clear in order to search for any other sails. In port, their duty was to tally the cargo as it was discharged. In return, they might be taught such essential skills as navigation and rope work, such as splicing and knotting.

Middies' recreation came when the ship was becalmed and they were allowed to launch a boat, swim and fish. They also fished over the side of the main ship for bonito and shark; any catches were a welcome addition to the daily meals on board. Aboard ship, they were allowed to put on theatricals and concerts and also had sporting events, such as scaling the mast and swinging down on the ropes,[29] or wild races, as described in the diary of the 1886–1887 voyage by Edward Fuller.

Hammock-men

'Hammock-men' (possibly ship's boys, Lubbock gives no details of who they were) assisted the middies by stowing the hammocks when not in use, washing their clothes, cutting their hair and generally attending to their wants and needs for the sum of £1 per middy per voyage.[30]

Carpenter

The carpenter was the senior officer forward and took orders from the officers but otherwise was mainly independent, though he would assist when the call was 'All hands on deck'. On Henry's 1882 voyage on the *Superb* the carpenter was one John Yule, 'Chips', who was described as being much sought after and doing everything in a good workmanlike manner, even fixing trunks in the cabins in preparation for the rough weather, making bookshelves and being very obliging.

Boatswain

The boatswain was basically a foreman, superintending practical work such as cleaning or painting. In the 'All hands' situation, his place was on the foremast. On the 1882 voyage, the position was held by Corbett, a man with great experience in the company, having previously served under Henry on the *Highflyer* and for five voyages on the *Superb*.

Sailmaker

The sailmaker carried out his work under the chief officer but in a largely independent way, like the carpenter. On the

1882 voyage the sailmaker was G Matson, 'Sails', who had been on board the *Superb* for five years and had a reputation for ornamental rope work, as well as being regarded as a well-read man and a poet.

Engineer

The engineer on the 1882 voyage, presumably in charge of the condensing engine, was Richard Pyburn. He could make a ring out of a shilling.

Quartermasters

The three quartermasters between them steered the ship in a ceaseless cycle of two-hour shifts. The editor of the *Superb Gazette* in 1882[31] made a particular point of mentioning them, having spent some time talking to them. One, Silva, had been with the company for 18 years, and doubled as the ship's barber, cutting hair and shaving beards, and doing the washing for some. A second, Mersey, was 'the true type' (I think the writer in the *Gazette* means a 'genuine sailor') at the helm, while in his spare time he played the fiddle for the hornpipe and other dances on deck. He also took care of the middies. The third man was Bailey, one of the oldest servants of the company. 'What a jolly Neptune he made, and how well he looks at the wheel, in his coat of many colours, like Joseph. Everybody likes Bailey, and calls him a jolly good fellow.'

Ordinary seamen

The ordinary seamen worked on the constant greasing and tarring that took place on board. The lowliest rank on board, they slept in hammocks on the lower decks where it was dark.

The cook, head steward and kitchen hands

Occupying the galley and tasked with feeding both passengers and crew, the cook had to tend to the cooking fires in the galley, and maintain the pans, boilers and utensils that were necessary for preparing many meals. The kitchen hands assisted with meal preparation, and the stewards took the food to the passengers, serving those in first class. On Henry's 1882 voyage, the head steward (name unknown) was a man of great experience who had been with the company for 17 years, nine of those spent on the *Superb*.

Code of conduct

The Crew Agreement of 1880[32] listed not only the rations allowable for each man, described above, but also the terms to which every member of crew had to agree – namely, to:

> conduct themselves in an orderly, faithful, honest and sober manner, to be at all times diligent in their duties, and to be obedient to the lawful commands of the said Master, or of any person who shall lawfully succeed him, and of their Superior Officers, in everything relating to the said Ship and the Stores and Cargo thereof, whether on board, on boats, or on shore...

There is also a handwritten codicil to this agreement above Henry's signature on his agreement:

> The said crew shall forfeit to the owners the sum of ten shillings each man not joining the ship at the East India Docks. The Steward and servants to be responsible for the safe delivery of the plate and cutlery at the end of the voyage. Each man to provide himself with a hammock and attend Divine Service when required.

Clearly Henry's men aboard the *Superb* met the mark, since it was said in the ship's paper in 1882: 'I think we might go on many a ship and not find a better captain or a better set of sailors.'[33]

The watches

The editor of the *Superb Gazette* in 1882[34] outlined the usual routine on board. The structure of the day was maintained by the ship's bell that was struck to mark the time and the change of watches. The nautical day went from noon to noon, the new day being heralded by the bell being struck eight times at noon. At 12.30pm, the bell was struck once, at 1pm, twice, and so on, increasing by one chime every half hour until eight chimes were again reached at 4pm. At this point the afternoon watch was completed and changed. Then the same system applied for the first dog-watch from 4 to 6pm (the close of which was marked by the bell being struck four times); and the second dog-watch, which ran from 6 to 8pm. This was ended by eight chimes of the bell, after which the night watches, each of which lasted for four hours, commenced: 8pm to midnight for the first watch, midnight to 4am for the middle watch and 4 to 8am for the morning watch. The remaining four hours, from 8am to noon, were the forenoon watch. This system meant that an uneven number of chimes marked the half hour and an even number the hours, providing a framework of time for both crew and passengers.

Washing, hygiene and toilets

In her reticence, while Maud's diaries do mention her seasickness, they do not mention how she washed, laundered her clothes or went to the toilet. Roslyn Russell notes that the diaries she investigated were also quiet on these subjects, and she puts this down to the Victorian view that physical concerns were seldom discussed, being regarded as unseemly and boring.

In England during the 19th century the general standards of hygiene were minimal, especially for the poorer classes, consisting of little more than shared outside privies and running water at standpipes in the streets. Few people had baths. For the middle and upper classes there would probably have been a washstand in the bedroom and a chamber pot under the bed, and servants to empty and clean them. On board, some official records show that there may have been water closets on some ships, but for the steerage passengers who had been used to relieving themselves in the gutters these would have been a mystery. Toilet paper was not normally used; instead, sometimes, there was a shared rag soaked in vinegar to be used for cleaning oneself.[35]

Volo suggests that the captain's quarters on American ships may have contained a small privy, but whether this was also the case for British ships is not discussed.[36]

Music and other sounds

It would have been noisy on board: there was the rushing noise of wind in the sails and the snap of the rigging; the splashing of the waves rushing by; sea shanties when the crew were hauling on the yards with pipe and drum; the noises of the chickens and livestock; saloon passengers practising their operas, violins, pianos and flutes; the bell sounding every half hour plus the hours and the watches; the barking of orders and the tramp of feet on deck.

Blackwallers discharged (unloaded at dock) to the tune of a fiddle, their crews working the tackle and slings that hoisted the cargo on to the lighters alongside, while the middies did the tallying. Other ships were hailed with a trumpet.

Women's work

Maud often mentions her work on board, by which she means various knitting or needlework projects. Other accounts also note that women were engaged in handwork in the mornings, often reading in the afternoons,[37] and that captains' wives in particular brought fabrics and other supplies on board to keep themselves busy. For instance, one whaler captain's wife, Mary Brewster, discovered that she had made 600 yards (549 metres) of fabric into sheets, curtains, pillowcases and tablecloths during her two years on board ship. Other occupations included knitting (Maud mentions the jersey she is making for Harold), crocheting and embroidery to create items such as pipe cases, slippers and lounging caps for the husbands.[38]

The voyages of Maud Berridge

VICTORIAN VALUES AND THE ROLE OF WOMEN IN VICTORIAN SOCIETY

The embodiment of the Victorian ideal of the hard-working man, Anthony Trollope wrote *The Last Chronicle of Barset* in 1866, less than three years before Maud's first voyage on the *Walmer Castle*, working on his book early each morning before going to his day job as a postal surveyor in the Eastern District of London.

In a society dominated by males, such a tireless attitude to work – based on values espoused by Thomas Carlyle and John Ruskin – led to a widespread belief that a man's work should be well done and carried out with dignity, something that I think comes across in various remarks made by passengers about Henry as the ship's captain.

Victorian society was enamoured of the self-made man, and it was important for women to marry well in order to secure their financial futures. It has been suggested that Victorian gentlemen received a classical education with an emphasis on Aristotle's pagan virtues of justice, prudence, temperance and fortitude, while simultaneously espousing the Christian virtues of faith, hope and charity, and also being 'whole and unassailable in their practical wisdom and fortitude'.[1]

In return, these ideal men, at least in Trollope's novels, were often worshipped as gods or heroes by their wives.[2]

For instance, in chapter 19 of *The Last Chronicle of Barset*, Trollope writes of Mrs Crawley: 'that she could not endure to make him [the Reverend Crawley] think that she suspected him of any frailty either in intellect or thought. Wifelike, she desired to worship him, and that he should know that she worshipped him.'[3] Perhaps this view of an ideal wife's duties and attitude towards her husband at least partly explains why Maud endured seasickness so bravely in order to be with Henry on these voyages. Moreover, the style of Trollope's writing echoes the restraint and ambiguity that Maud also shows in her diaries: much is veiled and indirect, with the assumption that the reader will understand the subtext.

Maud and Henry also both clearly enacted their strong Christian (Church of England) faith by holding morning and evening Divine Service every Sunday on board, weather permitting. At these services, Maud usually played the piano for the hymns and listed them in her diary, as did the other diarists, Thomas Miller and Edward Fuller. At Divine Service they often sang the sailors' favourite, 'Eternal Father, strong to save, whose arm doth bind the mighty wave. Oh hear us when we cry to thee, for those in peril on the sea.'

Trollope died in 1883, the year Maud began her longest voyage, but the societal norms he both wrote about and embodied persisted long after his death. His influence and work had a more direct, practical application too: having been instrumental in establishing the postal service in Ireland and the installation of pillar boxes in Britain, his work greatly improved the system of delivering letters reliably and freely to little villages. This widespread postal network was something that would have been greatly appreciated by Maud and all the other homesick passengers on board ships, enabling the sending and receiving of the letters that were awaited so avidly when coming into port or crossing paths with other ships on their voyages.

Women on sailing ships
The Rime of the Ancient Mariner (written in 1797–1798) by Samuel Taylor Coleridge relates the unfortunate tale of a mariner who shot an albatross that had guided his ship out of dangerous icy waters in the Antarctic. Spirits then led the ship northwards until it became becalmed near the Equator in uncharted waters. In their thirst, the sailors turned on the mariner and tied the dead albatross around his neck. All the sailors except the mariner then died, and after some horrific encounters and the ship rotting and sinking, he found himself left to wander the earth for evermore, telling his story, still with the stinking albatross around his neck, as a lesson for others.

Coleridge wasn't himself a sailor, yet with this poem he tapped into and depicted the very superstitious life of seamen, in which the normal phenomena of the sea (winds, storms, phosphorescence and water spouts) were bestowed with malevolent magical powers and often blamed on women, as witches. Little wonder, then – as Dorothy Volo discovered in the course of her extensive research – that females were not popular on board. Despite this, there was a tradition of women at sea in the Royal Navy through the 18th and 19th centuries, though it was against regulations, on ships that were dubbed 'hen frigates'. Moreover, in battle the women would fight alongside the men as best they could, or assist the surgeon with treating the wounded.[4]

Prostitutes also went on board ships, though they seldom went to sea due to the fact that at the start of a voyage the sailors had probably already spent all their money, a scenario that gave rise to the Dead Horse ceremony described by Maud in such detail in the 1880 diary (see page 67), and by Roslyn Russell,[5] who shows a charming contemporary painting of 'Throwing the Dead Horse Overboard' (painter not specified).[6]

The majority of women allowed on board were warrant officers' wives, and sometimes the coopers, cooks and sailmakers were also allowed to have their wives aboard: women were 'an unavoidable nuisance'.[7] It says something that often women's names were omitted from ship's passenger lists, and their deaths were frequently not recorded.

The conditions for the seamen's women and children on board were even worse than those of the men: they had to share hammocks in the crew's quarters, and rely on their men to give them some of their food since they were not provided with their own rations. Their days were often spent in darkness below decks because they were supposed to keep out of the way until the evening, when they were finally allowed on deck to take part in any entertainment or dancing. Women gave birth in the dark below decks with little or no privacy or assistance, even in times of battle.

This lack of consideration for women carried through to land life, especially if the men were to die. Few benefits were available to sea widows, and often the regulations prevented them from accessing even the benefits that they were due, although some charities assisted them. Moreover, if a seaman died from his own actions, his wife was ineligible for any compensation whatsoever.[8]

The warrant officers' wives fared better than those of the seamen: they could share their husbands' cabins, perhaps had a little more money and could spend their time 'working' – doing needlework and knitting. In addition, they may have been allocated 11–12-year-old cabin boys to do their odd jobs, such as polishing shoes or assisting with cooking.

Finally, women whose husbands were of higher rank – ladies of quality such as Maud, the captain's wife – had a more comfortable cabin, a much better diet, and luxuries such as wine.

Despite the relative comfort of her quarters and conditions, life for the wives of the higher-ranking men was generally lonely. On board, Maud would have been socially isolated by the conventions of the time that would have frowned on her fraternising with the crew, excepting the steward and cook, or with men other than her husband.⁹ To pass the time, Maud undertook simple tasks such as copying out the log for Henry, as she mentions, and walking on deck with him when he was free.

Nor was life on a sailing ship fashionable. One photo of Maud on board the *Walmer Castle* shows her as a young woman wearing the formal crinoline of the time, possibly made from silk, but this obviously would have been impractical at sea, particularly when climbing up and down ladders, as she did from time to time. Indeed, in a diary entry made when leaving San Francisco she mentions that her formal clothes are put away and she resorts to something like a black woollen wrapper or work dress, shown in a later photo. She must have had some serviceable shoes too.

Given these privations, one cannot but wonder why Maud accompanied Henry to sea so often. The answer perhaps lies in the simple fact that they didn't want to be apart, a view that is reinforced by the following quotation from *Hen Frigates* in which Joan Druett cites one of her diarists, Mary Rowland, who wrote in 1873 of another Henry: 'As Henry says, we have only one life to live, and he cannot be at home, and it is very hard for us to be separated so much, and a very unpleasant way of spending our lives when one is thousands of miles away.'¹⁰

A ship's captain was well regarded in society in the mid-1800s; a master mariner, as Henry had become by the time they were married, could attain high status. Yet I think that the fact that Maud travelled so much with Henry indicates that theirs was a love match, rather than purely a respectable and prudent social one. Throughout her diary she records affectionate moments and small kindnesses by him: bringing her breakfast in bed when she felt seasick; reading her poetry up on deck by the light of the new moon. Considering the Victorian woman's way of minimising emotions and not mentioning the obvious in everyday life, one has to read between the lines. Reticence was an important virtue for women of Maud's social standing, making these observations all the more poignant and affecting.

Women's diaries of sea voyages

In Victorian times, letter-writing was regarded as a fundamental and practical attribute for women, whereas writing poems or treatises was regarded as a less useful or likely form of writing. As one writer notes: 'The epistolary style deserves to be cultivated almost more than any other, since none is of more various or frequent use through the whole subordination of human life.' The author hesitates, however, to expound any fixed rules, since letters are written on all subjects, and in almost every situation in which the "tide of events" can carry individuals'. However, she does suggest that 'ease and simplicity, an even flow of unlaboured diction, and an artless arrangement of obvious sentiments' are the qualities most required.[11]

While journals, scrapbooks and diary-writing are not mentioned in 'The Escritoire'[12] (a chapter in the *Young Lady's Companion*), perhaps there were fewer constrictions around this kind of writing because, unlike letters, there was no thought that they would be read by others: it was essentially private writing and not designed to elicit a response or convey, for example, either congratulations or sympathy.

The author of *A Victorian Passage into Time*[13] suggests that the Victorians did, though, have a few rules for diary-keeping. First, one must not attempt too much. This meant the writer should fit the size and importance of their entry to the size and importance of the topic. Second, any blank book would do, and third, it was indicated that being regular at diary-writing for a year would imprint the habit into the writer, as long as the entries were short.

Gypsy Scarlett, however, suggests that Victorian diaries were not private, as they tend to be now, but were instead seen as a way of recording and developing religious practice and to 'share observations with family and friends'.[14] As in speaking and behaving, reticence in diaries was valued.

Russell, meanwhile, purports that seaboard diaries served several purposes: they filled in time; they recorded a life-changing experience; they gave a moment of privacy; they were a vehicle for releasing pent-up emotions; and they provided somewhere to record philosophical or religious thoughts.[15]

Many of the diaries cited by Russell, in common with Maud's, include regular comments about the weather: it was of prime importance both in day-to-day comfort and safety, and as a reflection of how long it might be before landfall. Many entries note the prevailing wind – a fair wind was one that would blow from behind the ship and move it along in high style, while a head wind would impede progress. Latitude and longitude and distance travelled were also often noted.

When I first read Maud's diaries I wondered whether they might be more interesting to read and less repetitive if entries about such mundane details were removed, but on reflection I have left them in, since they are in many ways the core of the journey. They reflect a safe or dangerous passage, and the mileage each day was a reflection of the time the voyage might take, whether outward bound or heading for home, and therefore their notes were extremely significant to the writer.

The writing of Maud's diaries certainly would have occupied some of the seemingly interminable hours of idleness at sea, not only because they are long and quite detailed in parts but also because such simple things as organising pen and ink and managing to write legibly were rendered much more difficult by the motion of the ship. The substance of what she records contains little that is emotional or really private: perhaps this is Victorian reticence in action, or maybe some entries had more meaning to her than they do for the reader of today. There are many observations – she has a sharp eye for human nature – and reflections from time to time. A few of her comments may be seen as unacceptable and racist in the context of the 21st century: her attitudes to the Aboriginals or black people, for example, were part of the then prevailing British world view that measured other races against the British 'norm'.

In the migrant shipboard diaries of the National Library of Australia collection, Russell notes that men's diaries outnumber those written by women by about three to one.[16] This figure could be a bias on the part of the collectors, or it could be that fewer women had the skill of literacy or the willingness or facilities to write such long diaries.

There are, however, extracts of diaries by captains' wives in various publications. For example, *Annie Ricketson's Journal*[17] is based on the diary of a whaler's wife from New England who travelled with her husband as the only woman on board for three and a half years between 1871 and 1874. This was not that unusual: some whaler's wives accompanied their husbands because the ships had to travel so far to find the whaling grounds that their voyages were far longer than, for example, the two to three months it took to travel between England and Australia. Laura Ricketson Doherty's book summarises the diary entries without giving much of the original text, but clearly Annie had not had the educational background that Maud was fortunate to have had. There are many diary extracts, too, in *Hen Frigates*,[18] but I believe the length, depth and quality of Maud's diaries make them unique.

MAUD'S VOYAGES ON HENRY'S SHIPS

Maud made the voyage to Melbourne, Australia, and back to England on five occasions (1869–1870; 1880–1881; 1882–1883; 1883–1884 and 1886–1887) as recorded in the passenger records of the Victorian Public Records Office in Melbourne.

1869–1870 Maud's first voyage: the Walmer Castle
Maud and Henry were married on 26 August 1869 at All Saints' Church in Emscote, Warwick. Just ten weeks later, on 8 November, she boarded ship and at 7am the next day she set sail from Gravesend, with Henry taking the wheel for the first time as captain on the *Walmer Castle*, bound for Melbourne. The voyage took 73 days and they docked at Sandgate Pier in Melbourne on 28 January 1870.

The handwritten passenger list is available on microfiche at the Public Records Office, Victoria. The summary of steerage and cabin passengers gives 39 men (36 settlers, two gentlemen and one man in the army), all of whom were English (i.e. not Irish or Scottish), and one infant. The women were classified as spinsters above the age of 12, or as wives or ladies. However, Maud (a lady) is missing from the passenger list; wives were often omitted from such lists.

For their return journey, the *Otago Times* of 26 July 1870 records that the *Walmer Castle* had arrived in Melbourne on 28 January 1870, and was due to leave for London on 19 March (arriving at Queenstown, Ireland on 14 June), carrying the headquarters of the 14th Regiment of Foot's Second Battalion and returning to England via New Zealand. The British Army withdrew all troops from Australia in 1870.

Thomas Miller's diary
While none of Maud's diaries survive (if, indeed, she wrote them) for this voyage, we do have one written by a young gentleman called Thomas Miller, aged 31, who set out on this same voyage from London to Melbourne on the *Walmer Castle* to see the colony of Victoria. His diary is held by the National Maritime Museum in London.[19]

We know that Thomas went to school in Tunbridge Wells – quite possibly Tonbridge School, which had been founded in 1553 and was expanding in the 19th century in order to meet the educational needs of the Victorian middle classes for their sons.

Thomas starts his diary of the voyage with the passenger list, and rather disappointedly records that there were only two female passengers: Mrs Gilmore and Mrs Berridge, the captain's wife. The Berridges are listed as occupying Cabin 1, as would befit the captain and his wife, and he mentions just 12 other cabins: the saloon or first-class cabins. No mention is made of those in second or third class or steerage.

On 9 November, Thomas made his second entry, recording that the *Walmer Castle* was off the Nore.[20] They had left Gravesend with the use of a steam tug,[21] and had anchored for that night and the following day because of a dead fair wind that was unsuitable for crossing the Channel. Throughout the diary he copied the ship's log into his diary, recording the wind (force and direction), ships sighted, often the barometric pressure, latitude and longitude, and the day's run.

He was very critical of the food, recording that the biscuits were dry and the tea was more like soap suds. He was cold and miserable in the rain, wind and fog, and realised that the only way to keep warm was to go to bed. They had breakfast at 8.30am, tiffin[22] at noon and dinner at 3.30pm. The next day, he confessed to being most miserable: 'I am greatly disappointed in my fellow passengers, all of whom are invalids or old people going out to settle. The female portion consists of one old woman (who, however is the owner of a piano, so I must suck up) and the captain's wife who is generally invisible.'

Poor Maud, no wonder she was 'generally invisible': one can only imagine the culture shock and discomfort for a well-brought-up young lady arriving into the reality of life on board. And she was yet to really experience her *bête noire*, seasickness, which dogged her on all her voyages.

Thomas was very thankful for his Magee, an Irish tweed coat from Donegal, which proved to be as warm as three coats when on deck and served as an extra three blankets on his couch at night.

A few days later, the ship had started to rock: he noted that the ladies and children failed to make an appearance, and that even the captain did not come to dinner. He said he was not 'fit' himself, though he attributes it to the awful food and lack of exercise.

The pilot left on 13 November, taking with it all the letters that the passengers had busily written in those first few days. On 14 November it rained, and Thomas's cabin was soaked.

On 15 November, off the Eddystone lighthouse, a passenger who was going on the voyage for his health decided that 'the sea and his stomach did not agree', so he and a friend insisted to Henry that they should be put ashore. Doctor Hawke, one of the passengers, said he could die if he stayed, so a pilot cutter was hailed and the man and his friend departed the ship.

Thomas was invited into the midshipmen's mess, describing it as a cabin big enough for one and having four shared beds for the six middies (two were always on watch).

On 17 November the ship was becalmed and Thomas took some photographs. Porpoises were sighted at the stern all morning and when revolvers appeared, Henry made an objection to firearms on deck so only one shot was fired.

The wind then swung around to dead aft, and good progress was made so that they finally crossed the Bay of Biscay. Thomas approached Henry to ask permission to have theatricals on board, especially with Christmas Day in mind. Henry was enthusiastic: 'not only was it his pleasure to have them, but it was his duty to promote good feeling among the passengers and make them jolly'. After dinner, Thomas assisted in setting the stunt sails.

On Sunday 21 November Henry read prayers at 10.30am and 7pm and 'read them a great deal better than nine out of ten parsons one comes across ashore'. Thomas sees a thin streak of colourless light, a lunar rainbow.

On 23 November Thomas experienced a wet night because he failed to shut his port and shipped a heavy sea that wet his couch, and he had to sleep in the Magee. On this day the skipper's wife (Maud) finally appeared. The next day saw the middies making a row outside his window and squirting water into his cabin, and he had to administer a reproof with two heavy sea boots.

On 25 November the weather warmed up and the ladies appeared on deck once again, allowing Thomas to get at the piano for a tinkle. The ship's carpenter made him a bath out of a beef cask (better than getting up at 6am to bathe on deck) and he smashed his meerschaum pipe.

The following day he braved the mizzen top to help one of the middies, while an iron band fell off one of the yards on to the arm of a small child while held in his father's arms. 'The consequence is the poor little beggar has been howling ever since.'

By 29 November they were three weeks out and the weather was becoming unpleasantly hot. The ship and rigging were covered in red sand, thought to have blown over from Africa. Thomas lost his 'patent extra superfine tropical hat' overboard the first time he put it on, abandoned his black clothes for ducks[23] and canvas shoes, and slept in pyjamas for the first time.

The beginning of December brought lassitude and bad nights due to the heat, but Thomas was encouraged by Henry, who promised a good feed for all after the theatricals. The sea was calm and still and they were driven below deck by heavy tropical showers.

The hot weather brought short tempers: on 4 December there was a fight between two passengers, one a father of seven, who accused the other of insulting his daughter; on Sunday 5 December Henry disciplined a second-class passenger, threatening to put him in irons after behaving in a noisy, drunken manner.

On 6 December it was Dead Horse Day, an event that Maud describes in detail in her 1880 diary. It essentially involved the crew putting on a show to boost their funds after a month at sea – they had been paid a month in advance and through this performance hoped to top up their rum money. Thomas was working hard at the Christmas theatricals despite having been let down by some of the passengers, vowing: 'If I have to play [the piano] myself and act at the same time, I declare they shall come off.'

By 8 December they were only 70 miles north of the Equator, and the sea was beautifully phosphorescent. I imagine Maud would have loved her first view of this phenomenon, as she mentions it in her 1883 diary. Thomas was unimpressed by the show the crew put on for crossing the line, since they merely blacked the faces of two or three boys, then doused them with buckets of water to clean them up.

Another hat overboard on 10 December, which upset Thomas very much since it was a nice one that Henry had given him to compensate for the loss of the first hat. He wrote that he should have worn a hat guard, and that his face was now as red as that of a red herring.

It was not only Henry's birthday on 12 December but also that of someone not on board called Joe, who came of age on this day, and may have been Thomas's younger brother. Whoever he was, Henry and others drank his health with a 'flowing bowl' of 'chammy' at dinner. They did this at 8pm, the hour at which Thomas and Joe had prearranged to do so before Thomas set sail, although the ship was now two hours ahead of Greenwich Mean Time.

Rehearsals proceeded, with Thomas practising his piano parts and others learning recitations, such as extracts from Dickens (*The Pickwick Papers*). 'I am working hard now to get the rudiments of the music, and am prospering. I believe a fellow can do anything if he only has the pluck to stick to it.'

Thomas persevered with his photography, even to the extent of making silver nitrate with the help of the doctor since he had used up his supplies: a successful endeavour. The *Walmer Castle* then went neck and neck with a large ship called the *Thermopylae*, which had four staysails on each mast.

One of the mates, Nixon, reneged on playing his part of Mrs Bouncer, one of the main parts in *Box and Cox*,[24] until persuaded otherwise by the chief mate and a few others in a rowdy argument in Thomas's cabin.

On 21 December they had a really bad dress rehearsal and changed some of the cast, but there was excitement about seeing a shark's fin. A hook loaded with a piece of pork did not, however, attract it closer.

Many pigs and chickens were butchered in readiness for the Christmas festivities on 23 December, and rehearsals for the show went well.

The great day for the show arrived at last on 24 December, and amid the excitement two whales were sighted close to the ship. The show began at 7pm; an unfortunate occurrence, since they should have waited for Henry and Maud to arrive at 7.30pm before they began, thus demonstrating a lack of seagoing etiquette. After that gaffe, however, all went well, with *Box and Cox* getting rave reviews from the passengers.

Christmas morning found Thomas's cabin in a frightful mess because everyone had used it as a dressing room. The second-class passengers had promised a concert (of low music-hall songs), but it was cancelled because it appears they were too drunk to stand. Moreover, Thomas wrote: 'I don't think there was a single man – passengers or crew – who was sober and the drunken rows in the evening were something awful. One servant was so bad we had to put him in irons. I hope I may never see such a disgusting sight again.'

With damp and cool weather, things settled down, and on 29 December he wrote: 'I abstained from all stimulants today and as I turned in with a bad headache I don't think it can be good.'

Over the next few days Thomas wrote of making a wooden model of the condensing engine, practising a duet with Mrs Gilmore and unsuccessfully trying to catch albatross that were flying around the ship. New Year's Eve was quiet, as Henry had given strict orders against any noise because of the bad behaviour at Christmas.

The first few days of January were a mixture of calm and fresh breezes but strong gales sprang up and small seas were coming over the ship. One night they had a 'dinner dish of sea-pie – a concoction of everything, but awfully good' because of the heaving seas.[25]

By mid-January, Thomas was bored, even after much work on his model, and he took to climbing the rigging, finally reaching the trees.[26] They hoped to land before the end of January, travelling their furthest distance – 264 miles – on 18 January. He filled in the time reading *Handy Andy*[27] in his cabin, especially on dirty rainy days. 'The best meal I get in the day now is one of hot roast potatoes in the mate's cabin after tiffin, obtained for from the cook on the sly.'

A few events happened before they docked in Melbourne: Thomas sold his sea boots to the mate for £2; one of the crew fell from the top foresail yard but saved his life by catching the studding gear on his way down; 1,240 miles from Cape Otway there was a heavy gale; the third mate sent some middies up to the mizzen top to tie up Thomas when he was up there, but they didn't succeed; there was a collection for a purse for the captain that amounted to £15, to which Thomas reluctantly gave £1, thinking it humbug, though he did illuminate a testimonial to go with the gift; the ship was scrubbed and painted to look good when they arrived in Melbourne; and Thomas attempted to read up in the mizzen and again had to repel the middies who came to tie him up.

At last land was sighted on 28 January and the *Walmer Castle*'s name signalled to the lighthouse for transmission by telegraph to Melbourne. The pilot came on board and a government doctor checked everyone's health; cholera and other contagious diseases were a particular concern. Thomas mentioned the *Lady Jocelyn*, which was in quarantine with 400 migrants on board, and described both his emotions and the events that occurred when they reached land.

It is most splendid weather, only I am rather frightened with an account the pilot brought of it being 140 deg in the shade in Melbourne. Today being our last on board, we presented the skipper with a testimonial. Old Moore made the speech, which would have been greatly improved if he had been a little more generous with his H's. The skipper answered, saying, of course he had never had such a delightful set of passengers, and I led the musical honours.

10.30 pm We have brought up for the night, about a mile from the shore, and the ship at the present moment is in a fearful state of commotion – customs house officials, police ditto, and Greens' agent with an army of clerks, all assaulting the skipper at the same time. The agent brought letters with him, amongst which I was awfully delighted to find one from Joe. Such a lot of events have happened today that although I feel very knocked up, yet I am much too excited to go to sleep.

Thomas disembarked, decided Melbourne's hot weather was not for him and visited Tasmania before getting a passage back to England on the *Lady Jocelyn* because the *Walmer Castle* had been completely booked up to take troops back to England.

1880–1881 Maud's second voyage: with the boys
All that exists for this period is Maud's diary fragment (see chapter 3), which describes having both their sons on board with her on the *Superb*. There is no documentation of the date they arrived back in England (possibly mid-July), but we do know that Maud's mother died on 27 June 1881.

1882–1883 Maud's third voyage: records from the
Superb Gazette

For this voyage, the National Library of Australia in Canberra holds a copy of the on-board newspaper the *Superb Gazette* dated 24 March 1882, printed in Melbourne at the end of the voyage from London. The editor, named 'Hibernius' (presumably a saloon passenger), wrote of 'a journey to Australia in one of the most comfortable of marine homes'. The editor hoped for contributions of 'poems, short tales, parodies, songs (original), double acrostics etc., in fact any novelties calculated to make our paper instructive and amusing'.

On this crossing, DW Barker was first officer, FV Vale was second officer, MA Jones was third officer, and K Mann fourth officer.[28] There were 24 saloon passengers, 24 second-class passengers, a surgeon, 23 able seamen, two ordinary seamen, one carpenter, one sailmaker, one boatswain, one cook, one baker, one butcher, one engineer, one chief steward, four saloon stewards and nine midshipmen. Maud was listed first of the saloon passengers.

The ship left the East India Docks at 3pm on 10 March and was towed by two tugs to Gravesend, arriving there some two hours later. The editor wrote that it was impossible to sleep that night:

> The noises on board were of a most varied description, what with the trampling of the watch overhead; and the livestock on board, no doubt torn ruthlessly from friend and kindred, showed their indignation at such a proceeding in a variety of noises. Add to this list of midnight horrors the many steamers introducing at intervals shrill and agonising screams, and you have a full category of our first night's experience on the water.

The following day:

> A very dull morning, everything bustle and confusion, and all look miserable and seedy. Waiting for the remainder of the

passengers who embark here, or impatiently expecting the arrival of friends to bid a parting farewell. Tender came alongside about 1 o'clock; the captain and Mrs Berridge, who were lustily cheered, arriving soon afterwards. Weighed anchor at 3 o'clock, and proceeded down the river as far as the Nore where we anchored till 4 o'clock the following morning.

By 15 March, the passengers began to relax and a concert of songs and recitations showed that there was plenty of musical talent on hand.

The editor pondered on the vagaries of life on board – from basking in the sun on a calm sea, with all cares left behind, to the luxuries of having a piano, banjo, tambourine etc. available, as well as the human voice; and from the many books to read and various games to while the time away, to the situation in a gale and:

> the agonies of *mal de mer*. This may be very pleasant to the experienced seaman, who delights in braving the storm and feels all the better for a breath of wind, but to the novice it is simply detestable. Who then among the sufferers would not prefer to be on *terra firma*, seated by their own firesides.

He added a list of the other privations of being on board: limited living space; being cut off from supplies and left to their own resources; and being of necessity close to those you may or may not dislike. 'We should all be thankful that our voyage is in the good ship *Superb* with as jolly a captain as anyone could wish to have.' Various stories, riddles, acrostics and reports of on-board sports followed, including the discovery of four stowaways found in the coal-hole and the freshening sea in the Bay of Biscay that sent many to their bunks.

Maud and three others formed an entertainment committee and in due course there were concerts, including contributions from Henry: 'Captain Berridge next appeared; his rising was greeted with tremendous cheering, which was renewed after he had given a very feeling interpretation of "Home Sweet

Home". An encore was insisted upon, and he favoured the audience with "Juanita", a song he sang with much pathos.' Mrs Berridge was the accompanist and acquitted herself 'in a very creditable manner', and she also played the piano for the Sunday services. Other musical diversions included dancing by moonlight on the poop deck to an orchestra of one, a fiddler, and a sailors' concert that comprised a 'coloured troupe of minstrels', after which three cheers were given for Captain Berridge.

Other activities included the usual Crossing the Line ceremony (see pages 68–71), which provided a good laugh for all, followed by a sports day for the crew. The Dead Horse Ceremony took place one month out. More mundane trivia detailed included the fact that Henry was beaten at chess by the cook; both Henry and Maud were beaten in the second whist tournament; there was a sweepstake for the date of arrival in Melbourne; and the passengers began to use nautical terms in their speech.

By 12 May, with some 6,000 miles to go, the passengers were resorting to acrostics: here is the one for Henry (in imitation of Longfellow):

H earty and hale stands he,
E agerly scanning the horizon,
N ought for thunder he cares;
R egardless of storm or tempest,
Y ou see him at his post, in calm, fine weather, or danger.
B orn as 'twere to the sea,
E arnestly trying to speed us,
R ightly also, to a far distant shore,
R emembering the while dear old England;
I n health may God keep and guide,
D evoutly we pray to our Father,
G ood Captain Berridge so kind,
E ternal rest grant him hereafter, and calm fine weather in
    Heaven.

For Maud they wrote:

> M ay happiness your life endow
> A nd care to you a stranger be;
> U nclouded be that placid brow,
> D evoutly pray our Father we.
> B enignly may your life glide on,
> E ndeared to many hearts thou art;
> R emoved so very far from wrong,
> R egretfully from thee we part;
> I n more congenial spheres to move,
> D elighting hearts unconsciously;
> G od spreads over thee that mighty love,
> E xchanged but for eternity.

The sixth concert was held successfully, and again Henry sang 'The Whale' as it had been so popular last time, and he also supervised the spelling bee in which Maud came third, winning 1s, which she subsequently gave to the printing fund for the publication of the *Gazette* when they reached Melbourne.

After ten weeks on board, a second tug o' war pitted the saloon passengers against the stewards; they had previously been beaten by the middies. Again they lost.

On the Queen's Birthday, 29 May, a patriotic concert was held, opening with 'God Save the Queen', and during which Henry gave a spirited rendition of 'The Englishman'. In addition, they had a 'muster', all dressing up in various ways, including with a bath towel and a grand hat, and there were fanfares of trumpets to speed them on their way.

On 29 May a big sea broke over the decks, and the first mate, Mr Barker, was nearly washed overboard, with the ship rolling heavily. There was a lot of damage and the hen coops were washed down to leeward at the top of the ladder but were largely unharmed. Part of the main rail on the port side was torn up, but order was soon restored.

On 31 May the last pig was killed when they were just off Cape Leeuwin.

On 2 June, one of the passengers, a Mr Pratt, died from consumption, and a few days later a Mr Millard died also. Henry carried out the funeral services for both men.

Later that day there was a meeting about the *Gazette*, resulting in a committee being formed that included Henry, who spoke: he 'felt sure that all who had a copy would treasure it very much as a pleasing memento of a happy and successful voyage'.

The final concert was held on 6 June. Among others, Henry sang 'Isle of Beauty', and Maud sang 'When the Wind Blows in From the Sea' as a duet with Mr Sellen. It finished, of course, with a rendition of 'God Save the Queen'. The following testimonial to Henry was published in the *Superb Gazette* for the outward-bound voyage:

Ship *Superb*, 6th June 1882.
    Captain Berridge,
    Dear Sir,
    Before the termination of this voyage, which is now so rapidly drawing to a close, we, the undersigned passengers think it but right that there should be some public and general expression given to testify to you our warmest gratitude for, and appreciation of, your unremitting kindness to us, your attention to our comfort and wants during the time the good ship *Superb* has been our home, your untiring efforts to further our concerts, entertainments, and general amusements, in which you have ever been ready to take part when called upon, if your many duties would permit. In after years, when recalling to our memories the events of this period of our lives, we shall always link you with the most pleasant recollections. In bidding farewell, we all unite in wishing you health and happiness, and that you may long continue to fulfil the duties of the proud position you now so ably occupy. We would tender,

through you, our cordial and sincere thanks to Messrs. Barker, Vale, Jones, Mann and Doctor Connor, the officers of the ship, for the kindness and courtesy which have characterized our intercourse with them, and for the valuable assistance they have given us in various ways.

Lastly, but by no means least, to Mrs Berridge we desire to express the pleasure we have found in her company; she, with you, has been indefatigable in her endeavours to promote our happiness; and we trust she may long be spared to you in your voyage through life.

They docked on 10 June 1882.[29]

1883–1884 Maud's fourth voyage: her diaries
For these years there are the two volumes of Maud's diary (see chapter 7) recording the voyage to Melbourne and then on to San Francisco, returning via Cape Horn and Ireland some 14 months later.

1886–1887 Maud's fifth voyage
This was probably Henry and Maud's last trip to Melbourne. Henry died in 1891, so perhaps he was suffering from ill health by then, or had decided to retire since he was then in his mid-50s and he had been a sailor since he was 15. There is a family rumour that he had a failed lemonade factory in Leicester after his retirement, but no records are apparent.

Edward Fuller's letter
Edward Fuller, a young man, travelled to Melbourne on the *Superb*, leaving Gravesend at the end of November 1886. He described his voyage in a letter home to his family.[30] He does not mention his social status or occupation, but from the letter it seems that he may have been working his passage to Australia, perhaps to seek his fortune in the Victorian goldfields. For example, he wrote

of 'the passengers', or 'the saloon passengers', discounting himself, and he described some of the work he did assisting various members of the crew, including the stewards. He must have been under some discipline because he occasionally mentions time for 'lights out'. His handwriting is somewhat cramped, and while his vocabulary is good, some of his grammar and punctuation are not correct. He is a devout young man, enjoying Sunday worship and recording all the hymns that were sung. He was excited about his travels.

Many of his entries concerned food, including the first, which describes his dinner of roast beef and potatoes. He also said that he put on weight during the course of the voyage, so perhaps he was undernourished at the start. At the end of his letter he bid farewell to eight siblings, so clearly there were many mouths to feed in his family; no wonder, then, that food was such a preoccupation.

Only a few days into the voyage, Fuller describes how an ordinary seaman was lost overboard: the crew and passengers surmised that somehow he had broken a blood vessel because there was blood on deck, then had gone to sit on the bulwark (more blood) and perhaps fallen overboard from there. The same fellow had apparently only recently survived the shipwreck of the *Suffolk* off the Lizard Peninsula.

The Bay of Biscay brought many that 'queer' feeling, 'the ship seemed to be going round and round', but Edward was 'as hearty as could be' and still interested in food; he described how he and others were divided into messes where they received rations of flour, raisins, currants, butter, tea, coffee sugar, pickles, salt, pepper and mustard. He also details the usual meals: 'breakfast was porridge and cold meat left from dinner. For dinner we had salt pork and pea soup one day and [?] the other, also preserved potatoes and boiled rice.' And later, 'For Christmas dinner we had two boiled fowls, one leg of mutton and spare ribs, fresh potatoes, plum pudding and two mince pies. The dinner went down very well. At tea we had cake but could not eat very much.'

He particularly enjoyed various forms of sport, playing cricket quite often, and observing sporting events, including the Dead Horse ceremony and one to celebrate crossing the line:[31]

> Saturday afternoon the crew had sports. The first was the greasy pole, two tried but did not succeed, but the third climbed to the top and got a cheese. The masthead race was next. One race was to the top of the main mast then down again to the deck. Several of the crew went in for it and two of them had the skin torn off their hands coming down the back stays. The quickest time was 2 min 22 secs. The middies race was up the mizen mast then up to the royal yard and then down the back stay. Several of them had the skin torn off their hand and arm. One of them came down with a run and fell on deck but didn't hurt himself.

On another occasion, 'The saloon passengers held some sports to themselves on the poop but we were invited to attend.'

On a personal level, he describes washing himself on the fo'c'sle early in the mornings and occasionally washing his clothes, mentioning, 'I never wore any socks for weeks and my feet got quite brown.' He also notes that conditions in his cabin weren't the best: 'The rats run over me every night backwards and forwards to the store but I don't mind them now.'

On Christmas Day, despite no rough weather, the fore royal and fore-topgallant sails were carried away with a bang like thunder because they were old.

When they sighted Cape Nelson (off the Victorian south-west coast, near Portland), he said that it comprised 'low sandy hills and looked very barren. We had to go about at eight bells. The reason we go about then is so as both watches may be out at the same time. When we went about we were running away from the land and saw the Cape Nelson light astern.'

Edward's letter ended with hopes that it found his parents and siblings all well 'as it leaves me fat and happy as a king'. Obviously it had been a good voyage for him, perhaps a relief from the bleak slums of London, and who knows, maybe he found some good fortune in the goldfields.

Who cared for Henry and Maud's sons?

It seems that after her first voyage in 1869–1870, Maud stayed at home in England in their house, 11 Brooke Terrace, Milverton, Warwickshire. Harold was born on 13 April 1872 at Kenilworth in Warwickshire, and Jesse was born on 4 April 1874 in Leamington, Warwickshire. Perhaps Maud's mother took care of her and the boys during the two births.

The 1881 census shows Henry and Maud visiting Henry's brother Robert at 124 New Walk, Leicester. This census (possibly 3 April) also shows the boys living with their grandmother Elizabeth Timperley at 8 Aubert Park, Islington, London, where her status is oddly described as mother-in-law. At the same time, Harold, aged 8, is described as head of household. Elizabeth died at 8 Aubert Park on 27 June 1881 from hemiplegia, paralysis of half her body, so perhaps she had a stroke. Her son Frank was present at her death.

Harold and Jesse went to a day school, the City of London School at Blackfriars. Where they lived when their parents were away on board ship isn't recorded after 1881, when Maud's mother died.

THE PERILOUS JOURNEY HOME:
ROUNDING CAPE HORN

The bad reputation of Cape Horn rings down the years. With images of icy storms, icebergs, wild winds and huge waves in mind, surely rounding it must have been a source of anxiety for captain, crew and passengers alike at the start of the journey home, and a great relief to all concerned when they finally turned north for home after safely rounding the Cape. Successfully achieving this involved a dangerous week of vigilance and hard work for crew and captain, and seasickness and fear for the passengers, until the ship could pick up the north-easterly Trade winds that would speed them on their way home. Maud's diaries omit this part of the voyage, so three contemporary descriptions follow.

1870
Thomas Miller's diary described how his ship the *Lady Jocelyn* rounded Cape Horn.

April 19th, 1870:
There was more wind during the night and today than I have yet been in since leaving home. I slept through it all only having to get up once in the night to lash my [?].

Owing to the man at the wheel losing his presence of mind, the ship broached to, and the fore topgallant sail got torn to ribbons. I carelessly left my port open an inch and in the morning I found my cabin flooded. Lots of passengers were up the whole night, and the remainder did not get a wink of sleep. The wind is dead aft, and the ship is rolling tremendously. The thermometer was down to 36° in the night. A fellow tells me that at one time, when the man at the wheel made the mistake, there was a good deal of danger, as the ship was right down, bulwarks under. 304 miles!

24 April
Today, directly after they had started morning service, an iceberg was sighted ahead. It was a most glorious sight and is by far the most interesting thing I have seen since I started my journey round the world. Owing to the clouds passing across it, it was constantly assuming different shapes and shades, and when there were no clouds, the sun shining straight on it, had a most magnificent effect, making it shine and sparkle like a big diamond. Of course there was a great deal of excitement on board, the skipper leaving the service, and all heavy canvas being taken in.

Last night was a most fearful night, hardly a single passenger getting a wink of sleep, and many thinking at one time that we should run into an iceberg. About 3 o'clock the doctor came into my cabin with a most woebegone look, having been washed out of his own, and had a pipe with me.

26 April
The doctor came in about 2 o'clock this morning and informed me that Captain Heywood, who has gradually been sinking in a decline since he came on board, had died about an hour ago. The funeral took place about 12 o'clock, and struck me as being done in a very scurvy fashion. There was hardly any ceremony at all, his body being put in a common deal box and let over the side, while the captain hurried over a few prayers in the service. The doctor tells me they do it in a very different fashion in Greens' service.

30 April
Rainy, squally dirty weather. 240m

1 May
Passed the much-dreaded 'Horn' today. We are now in a great track of ships and sighted no less than 5 before

10 o'clock. I think the proverb of 'give a dog a bad name' is well exemplified in Cape Horn. The idea I had formed, from hearing it talked about, was – ships under close-reefed topsail or even bare poles – hemmed in on all sides by huge icebergs – never by any chance able to see the sun – and cold so intense you had to live in your cabin all the time. Instead of which the following is the case: fine fresh breeze with sun shining and ship going along under royals.

3 May
Run 340m!
  I did not get up till tiffin, directly after which I went on deck and witnessed a heavy squall strike the ship when she had her royal staysail set. The mizen topmast stay snapped about a yard off my head. I went to the wheel and gave a help as they could not get it round.

The skipper gave a champagne supper to celebrate the successful rounding of the Horn, and Thomas continued to record the minutiae of shipboard life (concerts, chess tournaments, the petty arguments and ins and outs of putting a ship's newspaper together, catching two albatross). He despised the skipper, Captain Reynolds, as an uneducated cad and refused to make any more effort with entertainment of any kind. They think they sight the *Walmer Castle* on her return voyage but it was not confirmed by signals because of some odd behaviour by the captain.

  On 12 July a tug came alongside with the Isle of Wight looming through the mist. The skipper permitted some passengers to go on board the tug so they could observe the *Lady Jocelyn* under sail. Thus ends Thomas's diary before he disembarked in England.

1882
Lubbock cites the log of an unnamed young Australian making his first visit 'home' to England as a first-class

passenger aboard the *Superb* in 1882 when Maud was on board. According to this, the ship left Sandridge Railway Pier, Melbourne, on 14 September 1882 with 12 first-class passengers and 55 crew, including four mates, nine midshipmen, three quartermasters, the 'usual' petty officers, engineers, 24 able seamen, three ordinary seamen and five boys.

By 23 September the ship had taken on a lot of water:

A terrible day and as bad a night. Captain [Berridge] says he never saw such big seas. Wind blowing a gale with furious squalls. Ship taking in water over all parts... About 10 o'clock a great sea came up astern and went clean over the poop: at same time the ship's head went into another big one, flooding the fo'c'sle, smashing the cuddy[32] in several places and washing some buckets overboard. Hen coops with contents all floating and sliding about the poop. On main deck seamen's chests, clothing and boots washing about ... The quartermaster was washed under the wheel and hurt his back ... all the men and midshipmen got washed out.

24th September.
Another awful day with furious squalls every twenty minutes ... ship rolling at 60° at times. No church but short service of sacred songs in the evening ... the seas are terrible. I don't like looking at them at all.[33]

The journey ended safely even though there was a near collision with another ship, and there was also a sighting of the comet of 1882.

1882
Another account quoted by Lubbock comes from the unnamed keeper of an 1882 log from the *Superb*, which describes other incidents on the voyage that must have

been shared by Maud, including the comet seen on 14 November:

28th September.
We are to have a grand concert in the saloon on Friday, so today there are a few rehearsals, such harmony, especially of the quartette. It mustn't be mentioned though that I wish they would go somewhere else to practice[sic], the voices are all like lions, but a nearer comparison is like carrot grating.

2nd October.
The grand concert came off at 7.30 pm. The finest song was a duet, 'I Would That a Single Word' by Mrs Berridge and Mr Rowe.[34]

24th October.
Passed over 100 albatrosses resting on the water.

14th November.
Remained on deck until 12 when I saw the comet rising in the SSE.[35] In a short time it was nearly overhead. Its tail covered one-third of the sky. Its head was very bright and nucleus quite plain.[36]

16th November.
8 pm a heavy squall struck us and we luffed for a few minutes. The darkness was like a thick inky fog. Just as the darkness was lifting, a large ship, half as big again as us, came right on to us: she was reported by the man on the lookout when about 200 yards right ahead. Immediately she saw our lights, she put her helm up; she had all sail set and stood away to the southward. Everyone got a terrible fright.

23rd November.
Played against Rowe and Eden in a quoit tournament with the captain as my partner. We won the heat which made our opponents awfully wild. Concert held in the saloon tonight. Very poor indeed.[37]

6th December.
Saw the transit of Venus today through coloured glasses.

25th December.
At 12.30 at night made the Lizard lighthouse.

27th December.
11 am. The pilot came aboard at Dungeness. Engaged tug *Universe*, of London, for £50, to pick us up further on as we could sail faster than he could tow. 3.30, tug took hold. All square sails stowed away with a 'harbour stow'. Packing up has begun with a vengeance.[38]

So they were safely home just after Christmas.

1862
As bad as the *Superb*'s experience sounds, things were far more dangerous and difficult on the ship *Kent* when it rounded Cape Horn, according to Lubbock's description.[39] The *Kent* left Melbourne in July 1862 with 250 passengers and a full cargo of gold ingots, casks of sperm oil, bags of wheat and copper ore; the ship was overloaded. She began to strain and pumps were brought into use. Then:

> ... when the *Kent* was within 200 miles of the Horn, the glass fell to 28.10 and it was evident that dirt of the usual Cape Horn was ahead. In a very short while the wind was blowing with hurricane force, while a huge sea of Cape Horn greybeards threatened to wash the overladen ship from stem to stern ... Then shortly before dark a regular

Cape Horn snorter came whistling down upon the ship; and a greybeard came rolling up as high as the topsail yard. This sea struck the ship fair amidships on the port side and hove her down on her beam ends. The poop skylights were smashed in, and the poultry coops were washed down into the cuddy. The first class cabins were flooded, whilst drowning hens and wildly cackling ducks and geese swam about the flooded saloon.

The first-class passengers, seasick and in danger of drowning, were moved to some vacant second-class cabins with the assistance of the stewards.

Meanwhile it was going hardly with the ship. Things began to go and the great rollers of Cape Stiff began to loot the ship. The cow, house and all, went clean over the lee rail; the galley was washed out and reduced to a wreck; many of the men were seriously injured; and sails began to blow adrift from their gaskets and go to shreds, while the close-reefed main topsail blew clean out of the bolt-rope. It was a terrible night and Captain Clayton, who at the commencement of the blow had lashed himself to the mizen fife-rail, had the greatest difficulty in keeping his ship from being overwhelmed.

Just before daybreak there was a lull in the storm and the crew and some passengers were able to open the hatches. They tossed copper ore and bags of wheat overboard but still the ship was straining badly. The next to go was the sperm oil, which was pumped out to canvas bags hung out to windward. The bags were pricked so that the oil dribbled out. This had the desired effect:

The result of using the oil was instantly perceptible. The Cape horn greybeards ceased to break within the range of the oil. Yet as the ship, which was, of course hove to, slid down into the trough between each of these hills of water, the sperm oil like congealed fat was blown over her, torn from the crests of the seas by the hurricane, until everything reeked of whale oil from the lower mastheads down. And weeks afterwards, when the ship had reached the tropics, the oil still dripped from aloft to the vast discomfort of those on the deck beneath.[40]

PART 2

Maud Berridge's travels in her own words

3

On board with the boys

The passenger list, crew releases and cargo records for the *Superb*'s 1880 and 1883 voyages are kept in the Victorian Public Records Office in a quiet street in North Melbourne. A pleasant building with a café that looks out on to the leafy street, there's relatively high security to get into the reading room. The cargo lists need to be brought up from the basement, as do some volumes of the crew release records at the termination of their voyages. The crew names are written in a heavy landscape book titled *British and Foreign*, which features black cloth on the end boards and has tooled leather binding for the spine. There are marbled endpapers with a blue background like corrugated iron covered by a spidery red, yellow and black design. All the entries are in varying degrees of copperplate, and there's also the spidery handwriting of an 11-year-old boy named Henery [*sic*], whose mark is an X, and at the front is a list of ships' names. In both 1880 and 1883 there is no record of seamen leaving the *Superb*, but many other crewmen were released at the termination of their voyages, possibly to seek their fortune in the Victorian goldfields. Wages seem very low. For instance, one George Roper, an AB [able seaman], was paid out on 10 July 1883 for his work on board from Liverpool to Melbourne the princely sum of £3-4-00. If he had been a cook he would have received an extra 15s 6d, while an ordinary sailor received £3-13-6.

In a similar book, the cargo records are diligently written out. There is no record of the *Superb*, but many of the ships were listed as bringing 'sundries', presumably some of the comforts of 'home' not available in the colony, such as, I imagine, pianos, sofas, cookware, plates, cups, clothing and agricultural equipment. Perhaps also gold-mining equipment – the giant water wheels and water cannons that were used once the obvious alluvial gold had been picked up. Just down the road from my house in Castlemaine, the land around Forest Creek was at that time the world's richest source of alluvial gold, and not a kilometre away is sad Pennyweight Cemetery where the women and children were buried with just rocks to mark their passing: their funerals weren't worth a pennyweight of gold.

The passenger lists are on microfiche, the cards worn and dusty; so many people must have looked for their ancestors, just as I am doing.

For the 1880 voyage, the list records 11 1/2 adults in the cabins (Edward R and Mary Barnes, aged 38 and 34; John Vandyke aged 30; John and Mary Gardiner, aged 48 and 48; Bert McGovern, aged 6 – presumably the 1/2; Lilian Pringle, aged 11; Robert Blackmore, aged 35; Milton Parkinson, aged 21; and lastly Mrs Berridge and two boys aged between 1 and 13). There were also seven passengers in steerage, unlisted, so they must have had plenty of cargo to make the trip worthwhile: sundries, probably.

Apparently the crew liked having children on board and would make toys for them.[1] Certainly this is shown by the fun they all have with Jesse's fishing ventures.

Maud's diary fragment 1880
When I left London in my second voyage to Melbourne in my dear husband's ship *Superb*, I resolved to keep a sort of diary and got down the principal incidents of our outward passage, but nine weeks have elapsed, and from one cause or another I have deferred making a beginning until now.

On the morning of 22nd June 1880 I and our boys Harold and Jesse (my husband having necessarily started earlier) left our home in Highbury, accompanied by my brother Frank, his wife and her sister, my dear mother watching us sadly from the window. She bore the parting wonderfully considering her previous long illness. Still, only those who have parted with their near and dear ones for long months of absence and uncertainty can know the pain of such times. However, having once left home we were anxious to get to the ship. Laden with shawls, bags, etc. we took our places on the train for Blackwall and finally arrived at the docks. The two dear boys were delighted with the bustle and spirit that always marks the departure of a large passenger ship for some foreign port. Crowds passing up and down the gangway, either doing the voyage themselves, or seeing friends off. Arriving on board we found Bob, Georgey and their son Harry,[2] so with quite a family party to cheer us we left the dock and proceeded down the river as the ship made the first step of the voyage, so to speak. There was a ringing cheer from the shore, answered by the sailors on the fore part of the ship, as she slowly passed down the river in tow of a tug steamer.

The weather was dull and showery, but there was plenty to take one's attention in making speculations as to fellow passengers, and watching the passing banks of the river, which however are not very pretty in that part. One pretty incident occurred as we passed the training ships *Chichester* and *Arethusa*: a little sailor boy on board the *Superb*, who had been on the former ship and [was] going on his first voyage, mounted the rigging, and standing on the yard arm waved his cap three times. In a moment the rigging of the *Chichester* was covered with his old shipmates, and as the *Superb* came alongside, they gave our little man a hearty hurrah, after which he at once descended to his work in a matter-of-fact way. In appearance he is the very type of an English sailor boy, and I could not help wondering what his future life would be, left entirely to his own guidance, or the influence of the sailors he happens to be thrown amongst, for as a rule these boys are without family or affections, having been picked up from the streets.

We arrived at Gravesend about 6 pm, when a few other passengers came on board, also my husband, who had remained in London on business and came to Gravesend by train.

There were different reports as to whether we should remain off Gravesend all night or proceed at once to sea. The latter proved to be the case, and this was the signal for our friends to depart. Our goodbyes over, we watched the boat that took them to the shore and tried to look hopefully to the time when we should meet again.

I then came down to our cabin and put our darlings to bed, with, I must say, very mixed feelings, but they were happy and bright, thoroughly enjoying the novelty of everything.

The next day I think everyone spent on deck watching the coast as we passed. Eastbourne I noticed particularly, as my great friend J G was there, and I knew would watch the passing ships with interest for our sake.

On the 24th June the tug left us, and the sails being up the ship was seen to advantage for the first time. We all watched the proceedings with great interest and that as the ship began to <u>sail</u>, certain internal sensations made us aware, or some of us, that we were indeed on the Briny Ocean! Night came on, and the most extraordinary babel of sounds seemed to be going on overhead, as I lay in my <u>swinging</u> bed: flapping of sails, pulling of ropes, shouting and singing of the sailors with trampling feet. Added to the fact that <u>everything</u>, oneself included, was swaying and swinging about, made sleep seem very far off indeed! However the noises in due time became familiar, and *mal-de-mer* is of short duration to most people, to which I am an unfortunate exception. I will only add on that subject that I have been weeks recovering, but most of the other passengers are well and on deck again in a few days.

I watched the pilot take his departure from my cabin window. He had with him a budget of letters to post on his return to land, with which we had broken the last link until, please God, we arrive at the other end of the world, Australia.

There are fourteen passengers, only three ladies beside myself, and a little girl about 12 years old[3] on her way home from Germany. She is supposed to be under my care, but shares the cabin of another lady and seems happy and very good. I have often listened to tales of life in Fribourg, and little snatches of German songs she can remember, and how she had to listen to the beautiful music of the Roman Catholic cathedral, but as I heard a [?] declare, 'I am digressing!'

Nearly every morning I managed to get on deck, with the help and care of dear Harry, who is most patient with all my whims and fancies, which I know are many, during that most awful, indescribable sickness!

As we passed the island of Madeira (which we passed 8th July), the climate becomes every day more delicious: bright sun, blue sea, and such starlight nights, that it is with difficulty we can make up our minds to go down to bed. Some of the gentlemen are up again at sunrise and indulge in saltwater baths on the poop in very negligé costumes, I hear. The ladies come up after breakfast, when the awning is spread. Easy chairs and yellow-backed novels are the prevailing taste: white hats, coats, shoes, puggarees,[4] thin dresses and parasols added to the blue sea spreading all around. Snow white deck, rigging and sails of the ship, and the dim outline of Madeira on the horizon form a very pretty picture. We all seem thoroughly to enjoy the existence so free from care, we have been taken to another world where the sun is always shining, and the sea always calm. The Captain however does not appreciate too much of the latter and longs for a breeze. The days are getting too hot now for the gentlemen to continue their games of cricket and quoits. The twylight[5] is very short.

10th July

We passed the island of Palma, not particularly interesting that I am aware of, beyond the fact that it is <u>land</u>. We have spoken[6] a few ships so far.

July 17th

[Today] was again lovely in the morning. I took some pictures on deck to put into the boys' scrapbook, and also commenced a bag for Harry's pipes. The heat gradually increased, and I felt obliged to go below and lie down, feeling quite done up. However my headache (which was intense) accompanied by distressing sickness <u>increased</u>. Our Doctor was very kind and attentive, and finally administered some Chloroform, which sent me into a delicious sleep. I did now quite recover for a day or so, and I think I may have had a slight sunstroke, as it was a totally different illness to any I ever had before.

We are now looking forward to a ceremonial called by the sailors 'Burying the dead horse'. Having received a month's wages in advance before leaving home, the day that month expires is celebrated by a holiday being given to the men. In the evening our attention was attracted by a chorus sung by the sailors. Looking over on to the main deck, we saw them issuing in procession from the fo'c'sle: one or two boys carry-ing lanterns, then came (seen by the dim light) was a capital representation of a horse, made of canvas, with flowing mane and tail of oakum, his flashing eyes we afterward heard were the bottoms of soda water bottles! Riding the steed was a jockey, rather a good-looking young sailor, with a striped jersey, peaked cap, white inexpressibles[7] and top boots, also a whip which he cracked from time to time in unison with the chorus. Having brought the horse, which was rather restive, to the foot of the poop steps, a singular-looking individual with a mask and a long white beard mounted a barrel and put the horse up for auction. There was spirited bidding among the passengers, the money afterwards being distributed among the men. The horse in the meantime, with the jockey still on its back was hoisted to the yard arm, and amidst cheers and the burning of blue lights, he was cut away and fell into the sea with a great splash, the jockey of course taking care of himself, we soon saw him come safely down the rigging and could not but admire his get-up. There was afterwards a good deal of singing on the main deck, accompanied by a violin and a cornet. I may mention this took place July 22nd.

We now began to look forward to 'crossing the line' and vague hints were thrown out as to the probability of Neptune coming on board, which I think made a few have inward tremors and doubts as to how they might fare in the shaving process.[8] Jesse had been very anxious to fish over the ship's side so was allowed as the weather grew calmer to provide himself with a string with a bent pin on the end. To his great astonishment he caught a <u>red herring</u>, and continued fishing for days, during which he caught various treasures: an old watch guard, a packet of goodies, empty tins and bottles, never in the least suspecting that his line hung just over the <u>Steward's cabin window</u>, who amused himself tying things at the end, which caused great delight to the boys and amusement to us all.

July 30th

We were discussing the probability of crossing the line the next day. The wind was so light that we were making very short runs. About 7 pm when sitting on the poop in the delicious starlight, we heard a sudden cry of 'Boat Ahoy!' At such an unusual sound we all sprang up and looked over the ship's side to see the arrival of Neptune's Secretary. He presented a very strange appearance, having a large white fur cap which nearly covered his face leaving only a long thin nose looking pinched by cold, and a flowing white beard visible. His costume was an immense overcoat, carrying in his hand a portmanteau which we were told contained letters from His Oceanic Majesty. Four sailors in oilskins and sou'westers with lanterns in their hands accompanied him onto the poop. We all pressed forward for an introduction to the Secretary. After a great deal of handshaking the letters were delivered and we were given to understand that Neptune himself would honour us with a visit the next day. Then came goodbyes, and as they all looked so cold and expressed great fatigue with their voyage to the ship, they were refreshed with a little rum! Then the departure and in a moment we saw a bright light floating rapidly away to sea, which we were told was the boat returning – (but a little bird whispered afterwards that it was a bucket of lighted tar!). We watched it sailing further away for about quarter of an hour, then turned our attention to the letters we had received. Mine is a fair specimen of the letters, though of course they varied, so I will copy it here.

Oceanic Palace July 1880
    Mrs Berridge
    I have heard long since that you were coming out with your husband, my old friend Captain Berridge, and as the good ship *Superb* has arrived at last near my habitation where I hold full sway, I shall pay you a visit tomorrow, and I shall be most happy to welcome you here, and count you one of my numerous friends.
    Until we meet!
    I remain your well-wisher and allow me to add, friend
    Neptune
    King and Ruler of the Sea.

This of course gave us a great deal to talk of, and we went to bed anticipating the visit of His Majesty.

July 31st
Another lovely morning, but fortunately not so hot as it has been. Soon after breakfast, strains of 'Rule Britannia' from the main deck warned us that Neptune was on his way. Neptune

(personated by an immense sailor) was seated on the gun carriage, his legs and arms painted a red-brown, through which the tattooing was clearly visible, a silver (!) crown on his head, a trident in his hand, a flowing sort of garment which made a fine display of his enormous arms and legs. Seated by his side was Amphitrite, carefully carrying a baby, becomingly dressed in feminine attire with flowing hair and sparkling earrings. They were drawn by four Tritons in harness.

Attending their Majesties was quite a large suite: the Wandering Jew, the Doctor, his assistants, Barbers and Policemen, all in elaborate costumes representing their vocation. After their presentation to the Captain, amid some jokes and fun at the Tritons, came the serious business of shaving, our boys being the first victims, looking rather dubious but on the whole acquitting themselves very well. Harold's chief objection being to kiss the baby, as he was told to do afterwards because its <u>face</u> was <u>rough</u>! All went through the same ceremony as nearly as possible, which I will try to describe.

We stood on the poop in a group, then the four policemen came solemnly up the steps with a writ, on which was inscribed the name of the next victim, who was then marched off to shake hands with Neptune, who was by this time sitting in State. Then taken to the Doctor who felt his pulse and administered a horrid-looking though harmless mixture out of a bottle, then he had to sit on a raised seat with his back to a sail full of water about four feet deep. The barber then arranged his hair with a broom, shaved his chin with a series of razors each about a yard long, after using a great deal of lather out of a bucket; asked him many questions, the moment the patient's mouth opened to reply, the lather brush was popped in, and he was sent backwards into the water where the four Tritons awaited him. After a few dips, he gladly made room for the next one.

All that created great amusement to the spectators and everything passed off good-temperedly.

After dinner came athletic sports, with prizes and money for each and never shall I forget the treacle tin process, which was on the principle of bite-apple: with buns smeared with treacle hung on a string, as each man opened his mouth for a bite, into which Mr Lee (3rd officer) popped a spoon full of treacle, which as often as not alighted on the eye or the nose of the individual, then the pantry boy threw flour and the effect may be guessed as each man's face became gradually covered with the two ingredients. In the evening a concert was held given on the main deck, by some Minstrels with very white shirt fronts and very black faces. Altogether we passed a very amusing day and felt that we had made a break in the voyage, having crossed the equator.

At times we have seen porpoises, grampuses, and the lovely little Portuguese Men of War (Nautilus), which look like miniature ships of a pink colour in full sail. The most wonderful and beautiful phosphorescent light is seen in the wake at night, looking over the ship's side one sees all sorts of fantastic shapes in the brightest silver, the wake of the ship looks like a broad pathway of molten silver.

However, we gradually left these tropical signs, and a very marked change in the temperature soon made us don warmer clothes, dispense with the awning on deck and altogether convinced us of a decided change of climate. It was now proposed that some weekly concerts should be got up. The first took place August 1st, the performers being chosen from the 1st and 2nd class passengers and sailors and was great fun. My husband being Chairman, the Doctor got up a splendid programme with a clever comic etching at the top. One of the sailors opened the concert with 'Tennessee'. At the end of the first line, being rather nervous, he came to a full stop, and said, 'I knew I couldn't do it'. However, with some encouragement and cheering he began again and succeeded. There were some good readings, too, Harry sang 'The Whale' and the concert concluded with 'God Save the Queen'.

At the following concerts some of the performers sang in character, which added considerably to the amusement, especially 'Two Obadiahs' by Mr Barker and Mr Barrows. Mr Barnes took the Chair on one occasion, as the Governor of Tristan da Cunha (as we were just off that island). He was a very dandy Frenchman, his shirtfront elaborately ornamented with sea birds and reptiles, again the doctor's handiwork, who is so clever with his pen. Mr Lyte read 'The Pied Piper of Hamlyn' in a startling and becoming costume of red and yellow, flowing flaxen hair tied back under a black skullcap. Harry sang 'Isle of Beauty', which I accompanied on the piano, he was rapturously encored!

August 8th

It is now too cold to sit long on deck, and we ladies cannot manage much walking as the ship is rolling a great deal. We look forward to rounding the Cape of Good Hope, that we have fair winds. Some days I get to the dinner table, when one's head is not steady, it is trying, to say the least, to see things wobbling (that is a word invented on board as being very expressive!).[9] Legs of mutton slide off the dish, the stewards appear to be staggering without aim or object, and we frequently have to clutch our plates or glasses frantically to prevent them coming to an untimely end!

August 17th

We have had some terrible rolling the last three days and nights. No one is able to sleep or in fact do anything but hold on! The ship pitched and lurched so violently on this day that my husband said I and the boys must remain in bed, as being the safest place. Strange to say Harold (8) and Jesse (6) do not seem to have the slightest fear though the circumstances are most unusual for them. The deadlights being closed, the cabins are almost in darkness. There is a fearful sea running and the ship seems a mere toy with the force of the waves.[10] The breakfast things were rolling about, a lurch sent a basketful of forks, spoons etc. into our cabin off the table, the porridge was swamped on its journey from the galley to the saloon. I can give no idea of that dreadful day! Every hour the weather seemed to grow worse, and about midday the ship was 'hove-to'. Enormous waves...

And here the fragment ends, with the 17 August entry written on a spare page at the front; it seems she had run out of blank pages. We know of course that they did arrive safely because she lived to tell the tale!

4

To Melbourne, then off to San Francisco

It was 1883, and having left London for Melbourne on 12 February 1883 with migrants and travellers on board, and a cargo of 'sundries', the *Superb* arrived in Melbourne on 21 May (67 days at sea).

The passenger list for this voyage is listed in Appendix III as 20 saloon passengers and 14 in steerage. The crew was not recorded for the first part of this 1883 voyage, but it was probably similar to that of the 1882 one mentioned earlier. The *Superb Gazette* of 1879[1] has similar figures for the crew, so it is likely that they would have been much the same for the 1883 voyage.

In Melbourne Henry received orders not to return directly to London, but to instead pick up a load of coal in Newcastle, NSW, and take it to San Francisco. Following that he was to take on a load of wheat in San Francisco and transport it to County Cork in Ireland.

Maud and Henry stayed in Los Angeles for two months, waiting for the southern summer to unfold, and then sailed home down the west coast of the Americas, around Cape Horn, and north towards Ireland, whence they had the relatively short journey to Acton in London, their home. The whole journey took 14 months to complete, and Maud recorded it in her two diaries: one from London to Melbourne, the other from Melbourne to San Francisco and back to London.

MAUD'S 1883–1884 DIARY

Diary of a voyage from London to Melbourne
  By Maud Berridge, wife of Captain Henry Berridge
  Beginning 12th February 1883
  Ending 21st May 1883
  From Melbourne to Newcastle NSW
  Beginning 14th June 1883
  Ending 21st June 1883
  From Newcastle NSW to San Francisco California
  Beginning 13th August 1883
  Ending 2nd October 1883
  and
  From San Francisco to England
  Beginning December 6th 1883
  Ending April 1884

February 12th 1883
This morning I took the first step (so to speak) of my fourth voyage to Melbourne. G. came on board with me at about 12 am with the hope and intention of setting our cabin straight, but really on our arrival it appeared a perfectly hopeless task: boxes, cushions, chairs and brown paper parcels seemed to fill every available space. However, after a struggle of two or three hours I knew where <u>some</u> of our things were, and Harry² told the Steward to make up the bed and lay the carpet, which improved matters. During the unpacking several friends came in to say Good-bye, at last the signal was given for visitors to go on shore, and then came the final leave-taking. We all stood on the Poop waving hands and handkerchiefs to the group on the dockside who stood watching us as the Tug took the ship slowly out. The rain was pouring down and everyone looked and I believe felt thoroughly miserable. One gentleman friend shouted to me, 'Goodbye. Now I'm going home to sit down by a nice comfortable fire!'

Harry was very busy arranging for our getting away. Somehow the interval between our leaving the dock at 1 o'clock and sitting down to dinner at 6 o'clock passed, and it was somewhat cheering when all gathered around the table by lamplight. Of course everyone is strange and stiff, a few quite at their ease, others glum, others painfully polite in attending to one's slightest wants.

There are about twenty-four passengers, only four of whom beside myself are ladies. Several I am quite sure are travelling for health, as I have heard from different cabins that dreadful tell-tale cough!³

One gentleman told me he had been paralysed by a fall from a bicycle, another is a dwarf and going on the voyage in the hope of growing!

The tug brought us down to the Nore where we are to anchor for the night.

Feb 13th

I went to bed very early last night, being thoroughly tired with the excitement of the day. In spite of the <u>hardness</u> of the bed I slept splendidly, and Harry could rest without anxiety, with two Pilots on board. Breakfast at eight – then a little more unpacking, fed my birds, a walk on deck till lunchtime. The sun is shining brightly but a strong head wind prevents our proceeding on our way. While the ship is steady I have taken the opportunity of writing letters for the Pilot to take on shore. A bag is hanging in the saloon for the reception of letters, and everyone is taking advantage of sending them.

Feb 14th

A strong gale blowing, and the water quite rough. One or two complain of feeling <u>queer</u>. No chance of getting to sea today. People beginning to fraternise a little, playing games, cribbage, backgammon etc., but pen and ink still in great vogue sending last words to those on shore. Our dear old dog Boxer slept in our cabin last night, and seemed so delighted, he misses home comforts – as we all do!

Feb 15th
We weighed anchor at about 8 o'clock and proceeded on tow as far as Deal, which we reached at about 3 in the afternoon. The weather still very boisterous, and the tide and wind being against us, we anchored until tomorrow. The first Pilot left us today, taking an immense budget of letters. I am writing in the Saloon at 9 pm. The lamps are lighted and the passengers are nearly all seated round the table with books, work or games. I have just played backgammon with a young fellow who told me he was going to New South Wales to learn sheep farming. The gentleman rejoices in <u>very</u> red hair and moustache, and he has already been christened 'The Golden Pheasant'. The dwarf has received the name of 'General'. All jokes at his expense he takes most good-humouredly and joins in the laugh.

Feb 17th
A day of miseries: the tug left us yesterday, so we are now sailing against a head sea and a head wind. Through the night it blew a gale from all around the compass in turns. Everyone is seasick. Only three passengers sat down to dinner making a party of six with Harry and the two offi-cers. One poor lady was seriously ill (Miss Bullions) with an affection of the throat to which she is subject, the attack brought on no doubt by standing in the cold and wet the day we left the dock.

Feb 18th
Our first Sunday on board. The weather is brighter and calmer. All the poor invalids struggled on deck except Miss Bullions, who is, however, better, and Mrs Benson.
    I wrote my last letter to our darlings, Harry enclosing a few lines. We are now off Dartmouth and only anxious to get a Pilot cutter to take our Pilot off. A blue light was burnt from the ship's side as a signal, but to no effect, so he will

spend another night on board, probably leaving in the early morning taking our last letters with him.

The moon is shining brightly and the water comparatively smooth. We are glad of a respite after the tumbling about of yesterday.

Feb 19th
The Pilot left us at 6.45 am, taking quite a large bag of letters, so now our last link with land is broken for a time!

Some of the passengers are reviving though most look very white-faced, and seem to hate the sight of the dinner table. Miss Bullions was better in the morning but seemed to have a relapse in the evening. I sat some time with her in the afternoon and she was cheered by talking of her married sister and little nephews and nieces.

Feb 20th
Harry has been up all night and we are now past Scilly, the weather is too thick and stormy for a sight. The sun did not come out till afternoon. I sat with Miss Bullions till dinner, she is not too well, poor girl and naturally depressed at being so far from home. After dinner walked on the deck till 7 and saw the moon rise. Came down to tea, sat with Miss B again till 9 when Mrs Wells relieved me.

At present I am thankful to say I have almost escaped seasickness, though how I may feel in the 'Bay' remains to be proved, but I am hopeful.

The 'Golden Pheasant' talks incessantly of 'ome' and his 'ouse'. Though evidently a well-meaning man I am really glad that we are not near neighbours at the dinner table. But it is too soon to judge character at present, but one I am quite sure will prove selfish and quarrelsome.

Feb 21st
A good deal of rolling through last night, everyone is recounting their experiences. The weather is brighter, and wind more favourable.

I put up a notice today requesting help to form a Choir for Sunday's service, practice tomorrow at 5.15. Miss Bullions is much better.

The *Polly*, a very pretty barque, passed us this afternoon, six days out from Liverpool, bound for Buenos Ayres [*sic*]. We had the great pleasure of re-passing her an hour later. The air is much softer now than when we left England, though there has been little sunshine, and both sea and sky look dull and grey.

Lat 47° 56' Long 8° 47'

Feb 24th
A lovely bright morning, came on deck about 11 am. Choir practice in the evening, a very good response to my notice put up in the Saloon.

Feb 25th Sunday
Still bright and sunny. A few gulls flying about over our head. Two ships in sight, one homeward bound, the other has been in company all day: the *Scottish Chief* bound to Queensland.

Divine Service was held in the Saloon at 10.30 am, a very fair congregation. Harry read prayers and we had the hymn 'For those at sea', also chanted the 'Glorias'. In the evening we had 'The Church's One Foundation' and 'Abide With Me'. After service some selections from the 'Messiah' played by a young lady. Also 'Nazareth' sung by a gentleman. We had to close the piano then as Mr Dale had 'turned in', however so far we enjoyed it.

Lat 45° 00' Long 14° 41'

Feb 27th
A dead calm, the water like oil. Harry out of spirits and everyone wishing we could get on!

Feb 28th
A fair breeze but cloudy. Two or three ships in sight, one very near. Worked away all morning at Harold's stockings,

had a nap. In the evening we formed a small party for cards, and I retired to rest at 10.30 after our little private supper.

March 1st

Quite an eventful day. Firstly a turtle passed close to the ship, accompanied by an 'old maid' (a fish) and a bottle covered in barnacles. We regretted afterwards not having tried to fish it up as it might have contained some ship's papers. Three ships in sight, one crossed our wake so near that we exchanged cheers. Her name *The Cambria*, from Scarborough, the *Meta* of Bremerhaven asked by flags 'if we had any ladies on board?' The answer being in the affirmative, the response was 'then we should be happy'. Rather a remarkable topic of conversation on the high seas, and with such means of exchanging ideas!

In the evening our first concert took place, and taken altogether was a success. One poor young man had to begin twice and failed at the first high note. Another gentleman sang a 'medley' and though the words were amusing, it would take an extremely clever person to make out the tune. Harry opened the concert with a short speech, and singing 'Juanita'. Being encored he sang 'The Whale'. There are rumours of a minstrel entertainment for next week.

March 2nd

Entirely calm. Sat on the deck at work all morning, read *Ivanhoe* in the afternoon. Played Dominoes and Cribbage with our General Tom Thumb in the evening. I really admire his character! He bears his misfortune with so much good humour and at the same time dignity. Poor little fellow, he has been suffering from chilblains so is unable to walk much on deck. It is really funny to see him poring over a book with the attitude and expression of a man, and he the size of a baby boy.

In the course of the day, six turtles passed us, floating asleep on the water, also a whale. Three ships in sight, but none homeward bound.

Lat 37° 31' Long 18° 16'. Distance 110 miles.

March 3rd
Fair breeze, though not very sunny in the early morning. It cleared about midday. I suggested getting up a quoit tournament so it has been a morning's work getting names. I have collected 28, so there will be six sets to begin with. Everyone is practicing [*sic*] quoits frantically. I suppose the [?] will last about a week.

March 4th Sunday
A delicious bright morning with a fair breeze, blue sea and Madeira in sight, but it only looks like a dark cloud on the horizon. Going on deck after dinner, we had left the island behind. We had service morning and evening.
    Lat. 33° 8' Long 18° 1'. Distance 163 miles

March 5th
Perfect weather. I helped Harry to copy out his log and list of passengers, and arranged with Mr Fendelow about a concert for next Thursday. Mrs Matthews came into the saloon to rehearse a song. She has been on the stage, and the manner is hardly suited to our small room, but her voice <u>has been</u> a very fine one, and if the song is not spoiled by manner, will be a great acquisition to the concert.
    After luncheon I spent an hour in unpacking thinner garments for the tropics. Dinner at 4 pm. Immediately Miss Bullions, Mrs Chermside, Mrs Benson and I secured four quoits and had three games as practice for the tournament. After tea we had a discussion at our end of the table on mesmerism. Then followed a very nice duet, violin and piano, Miss Bullions and Mr Warden. The latter is a youth with long flowing locks and a <u>yearning</u> expression of face. We were rather sceptical as to <u>his</u> musical powers, but were agreeably surprised. A game of Nap finished the evening with the exception of a short time spent over my diary.
    Lat 31° 21' Dist 108

March 7th

A very warm day. The Quoit Tournament began. We played on the main deck. Mr Carter, one of the midshipmen, was my partner and we won two out of three games and so shall pass into the next heat.

A small steamer passed very near to us about 8.30 am, but did not give us any information about herself. I began to knit a white woollen jersey for my dear sonny, Hal.

Lat 29° 15' Long 18° 33' Dist 37

March 8th

Another warm bright day, little or no wind. I helped Harry copy his log, and worked and read on deck. Very good concert in the evening, the gem was a lovely duet between the violin and piano. The former was played by a long-haired youth whom we had not given credit to for so much task and talent. His touch is really lovely and I look forward to the next performance with great pleasure. Harry is quite depressed at the continuance of light and unsteady winds.

Lat 28° 5' Long 19° 9' Dist 77 miles

March 9th

A great change in the scene since yesterday. We went to bed in a calm, hardly a breath of air, and the water like oil. This morning a strong southerly wind and head sea. Experienced some difficulty in dressing and soon felt queer. I struggled on deck where I found several others looking pale and shaky. Only about a dozen sat down to dinner, one or two made rapid exits!

I lay down all afternoon, read a little, knitted a little. Miss Chermside came and lay down on my bed for about an hour. I felt very pleased that I had played out the second heat of quoits, though beaten by one point. Went to bed very early and had a splendid night.

Lat 27° 12' Long 20° 20'

March 10th

Harry came joyfully into the cabin to tell me we had at last a fair wind! We have been a long time getting so far.

The last idea for entertainment is a Fancy Dress Ball so Mrs Leacock and I went round this morning to get names and costumes. If possible it is to take place next week. Brilliant sunshine and a strong fair breeze are really cheering. Great numbers of Portuguese Men o' War have been seen lately, they are very lovely. Also a few flying fish and one sea gull. The latter is supposed to come from the Canary Islands.

We passed a small brig lately pitching dreadfully in the heavy sea. We left her far behind, as she could not carry much sail. Our run today was 227 miles.

March 11th Sunday

Had service on the poop in the morning under the awning spread for the first time. While Harry read, the fowls kept up a most incessant chuckling and cackling, it seemed almost as though it were an opposition service in the saloon at 7.30. We had two pretty hymns: 'Weary of earth and fallen with my sin' and 'Hark, hark my soul'.

Lat 20° 37' Dist 173

March 12th

Four weeks today since we left London. The 'Burial of the Dead Horse' was carried out, which marks the end of the time for which the sailors have received money in advance. After tea we came on the poop. The stars were shining, but the night was otherwise dark. Soon we heard the strains of the old sing-song 'They say poor man your horse must die'. The noble animal, as he was afterwards called, came ambling out of the fo'c'sle, surrounded by all the men. The uncertain light of two or three lanterns and the melancholy tune they advanced by, gave rather a weird aspect to the procession. As usual the horse was put up for sale, and finally knocked down for £3.11.6, subscribed by the passengers as a present to the men. He was then hauled up to the yard arm, and by illumination of blue light was cut away and with a splash fell into the sea amid the cheers of the sailors.

March 13th
A good deal of excitement prevails today owing to the probability of our long talked about Fancy Dress Ball taking place tomorrow. Consultations are being held in different cabins. Mysterious parcels and garments are being carried about and exchanged. In one cabin I found 'Patience' very well represented by a pretty cotton costume and large straw hat, another young lady I had the satisfaction of converting into a very good imitation of a [?] peasant girl. My own costume is to be a German Fishwife, and Harry says it suits me very well. A little dance after tea.

March 15th
Still greater excitement as the Ball is fixed for tonight. Finishing touches are being put to costumes. I have sent out the various articles I have promised to lend, such as a scarlet scarf for a 'Hindoo'. Another for Bluebeard's Chamberlain, a white bodice for a Middy who is to appear as a young lady, also locket and chain, ribbons, flowers etc. About 5 o'clock preparations began for making the Ballroom, and by dint of enclosing a space on the poop with sails and decorating it with flags, a very pretty room was soon complete. Lanterns hung from above, and one end being open, we from time to time could see the open sea, twinkling stars and crescent moon hanging, so to speak, in mid air. In these latitudes the air is so clear that the stars seem suspended, but the tea is now waiting – and then to the Ball!
    Lat 14° 37' Dist 151 miles
    Having arranged myself as a Fishwife last evening and coming out into the saloon, I was really startled for the moment to meet face-to-face two brigands, a N_____, Arabi

Pasha, a Ghost and a Clown! Everyone was laughing and witnessing each other. The [?] was soon complete, and I with one of the Brigands (the Chief Officer) led the way to the Ballroom where we found Harry awaiting the guests. It really was the greatest fun possible finding out the different people. Programmes were filled up at once. The piano struck up a polka, and with the aid of two violins, dancing was kept up without the slightest intermission until 11.30 when we finished with Sir Roger de Coverley,[4] which I danced with a Red Indian!

A good deal of amusement was caused by the Clown running away occasionally with the Ghost, order being restored by the dwarf who acted as Policeman – he not being any bigger than a four-year-old boy! I danced every dance, and most thoroughly enjoyed the whole affair. Everyone pronounced it a complete success. After the National Anthem three cheers were given for Captain Berridge, Mr Barker, and someone kindly added Mrs Berridge, which was kindly taken up. We all then repaired to the Saloon for a little chat, and finally said goodnight about 12 o'clock.

Today of course we have plenty to talk of, and everyone is lying about the deck, and somewhat tired but after tea another impromptu dance was got up by about four couples.

March 16th
Getting hotter each day. Knitted in the morning, read and slept in the afternoon. After tea, dancing again on the poop. In fact having commenced dancing we find it difficult to give it up!

March 17th Sunday
Came on deck about 8.30 am thankful to escape from the hot cabin. Service on the poop at 10.30. I cannot understand why the fowls keep up such an incessant clucking and chuckling during the service, as though they all protested against it!

The ship is perfectly steady, the sun very hot but bearable by a nice little breeze which also takes us on our way. Lying in a lounge chair it is delicious to hear the gentle break of the water against the ship's side. The nights are now very hot, though we sleep with the windows open. The thermometer is only about 92° but the peculiar softness of the air makes it very oppressive.

Lat 5° 30' Long 21° 7' Dist 139

March 18th

Heavy thunder and vivid lightning during the early morning, accompanied by such rain as one only meets with in the tropics, coming down in sheets of water. About 11 am the rain ceased and everyone rushed on deck for air, where we found some of the gentlemen paddling about, the upper part of their bodies protected by oilskins and sou'westers, bare as regards legs and feet.

The heat was greater than ever, though the sun was clouded. I soon retreated downstairs again, but towards 12 o'clock the awning was spread. Again I ventured up and settled down with about a dozen others very comfortably for the afternoon with books and work.

After tea we had about an hour's dance by moonlight. Mr Schact brought up his violin for our benefit, as Mersey was at the wheel. Sat on deck till 11 pm.

Lat 3° 45' Long 20° Dist 105

March 20th

Woke up to hear torrents of rain pouring on the deck overhead. Oppressively hot, and I'm longing to go on deck. Continued rain prevents Neptune's Secretary coming on board this evening so the Sports must be postponed till finer weather.

I sat on deck for two hours in torrents of rain: rivers off the edge of my hat, and little pools every five minutes collected in my lap, but I really could not brave the heat of the saloon, so when thoroughly drenched I came down to bed.

A rather amusing incident occurred in the morning in the saloon: a young lady who had persistently sang and practiced [*sic*] every morning, somewhat to the distraction of the other passengers who were reading and writing, having had one's patience fairly tried by an hour's singing of vapid songs, the finishing touch was put by her commencing scales and exercises. One or two of the younger members of the community commenced to giggle, and finally broke into a chorus at which the fair cantatrice closed the piano with a snap and departed on deck to give vent to her injured feelings to a select few!

Lat 2° 37' Long 20° 53' Distance 69

March 22nd

Torrents of rain in the early morning but a temporary break in the weather invited the preparations for Neptune's reception. The procession issued from the fo'c'sle, Neptune and Amphitrite seated on a sort of triumphal car drawn by four bears who soon found their way on deck and embraced the legs of the gentlemen, sometimes rather too forcibly. Just as one victim had been shaved, a heavy squall came up of wind and rain and it certainly was a ludicrous sight to see the Barber, Bear Driver and Doctor pulling at the ropes and doing their ordinary work. The shaving was proceeded with afterwards, but the spirit of the performance was rather dashed by the rain. Though the awning was spread, the water washed about the poop almost as though seas had been coming over! The sports and concert are postponed for finer weather.

In spite of the rain the air is most oppressive, and no one can endure the saloon. The ladies take refuge in borrowed oilskins of their masculine friends, as ordinary mackintoshes are of no use in this downpour. The effect is very funny with hats and hoods over heads and faces. How I wish I could draw!!!

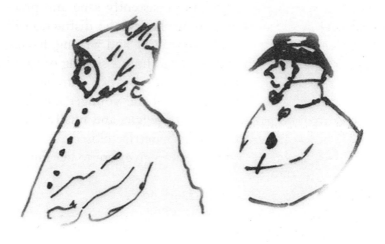

Maud's sketches of some of her fellow passengers.

Neptune's letter

Mrs Berridge

Madam

This is to let you know that I am coming up from down below to bid you welcome to these realms of mine although you have so often crossed the line.

Tomorrow morning, that is if all's well, I purpose coming on board so tell my old friend Captain Berridge.

I always pay compliments to gentlemen who come this way.

Tis many years since he and I first met
How many now I really quite forget
I trust that I shall find him well as yore
And hope to meet him many times more.

I hope you have enjoyed good health at sea
And that you've been from *Mal de mer* free
Tomorrow morning if the weather's fine
I'll call and bid you welcome to the line.
Farewell at present I must now depart
To hold my court on the Scotch Wizard

Hoping this will reach your hand quite soon
That hand I'll come and shake tomorrow forenoon

Till then

Ta ta

Neptune

March 23rd Good Friday

A day full of associations, even apart from its sacred character. Where are our dear ones at home? How often have we all knelt together in Church and listened to the solemn service! Harry and I read the 51st psalm together, and Collects for the day before coming on deck. It is a glorious morning and the rain we have had makes me appreciate being able to come on deck in comfort.

March 24th

The sports which were postponed from Thursday came off this afternoon and evening – racing, greasy pole etc., which occupied the whole afternoon. At 7.30 we took our places on the poop for the minstrel entertainment given by the men. The singing was not so good as on former occasions, but the step dancing and realisations were excellent, and altogether it was a success. Sitting on deck by moonlight and listening to the songs of the sailors was very enjoyable. The evening was so delicious that I stayed on deck till 11.30. There were rumours of a shark having been alongside, so the hook and bait were put over, but Mr Shark did not seem inclined to be caught. However about 12.30 when feeling very hot in bed and half asleep, there was a most unusual stamping and excitement going on overhead, and cries of 'We've got him!' Harry and I seized some garments and ran out on the main deck just in time to see the great brute come flop on deck – he was bounding and springing and lashing his tail. Everyone kept changing their position as the creature bounced about. There was quite an excited crowd, nearly every-one having sprung out of their first sleep. One man held a lamp over the shark, while another severed his tail with a hatchet wherein lies the chief strength, and with a sharp knife he was quickly dissected. I hear the midshipmen had shark steaks for breakfast this morning. His skull has been cleaned and looks like a curious carving in ivory. The jawbone is also hanging up to dry.

Easter Sunday

A real tropical day: brilliant sun, blue water. Service on deck at 10.30 and we sang one of the dear old Easter hymns, 'Christ the Lord is risen today'. After service, by special request, a boat was lowered so that some of the passengers might have a row. They soon found themselves so hot they were thankful to return to the shade of the awning. Luncheon over, it was suggested that the ladies might like to go for a row, so another party was made up, and we scrambled into the boat before she was lowered into the water. It was most enjoyable and we had a very merry party. The 2nd and 3rd officers with four middies came with us as one or two extra hands to take a spell at the rowing. A good deal of chaff and banter went on. I have never felt anything like the heat. The water was as smooth as a millpond with the exception of a long swell. Though we had hats and umbrellas, they seemed hardly any protection. The *Superb* looked lovely, truly a 'painted ship on a painted ocean'.⁵ It was the first time I had seen her under sail from a distance, and we were rewarded for the baking we endured by the novelty of the position and the view of the ship. Returning, the next difficulty was to get on deck again. We managed to climb the rope ladder at the side and quite a cheer greeted us as the last lady stepped on deck.

At 7 pm it seemed no one had the courage to go down into the saloon for Service, so Harry decided to have it on deck and by the aid of three lanterns we managed to see our books very well and finished by singing 'Son of my soul', the moon meantime rising out of the horizon and casting a long pathway of silver across the water. The Southern Cross is now visible and the dear old 'Bear' will soon be lost.

Lat 55'S Long 21° 49' Dist 26 1/2

March 26th
Came on board about 8 am and was thankful to find the awning spread. Still a calm, burning sun and great glare on the water. Knitting till lunch time, came on deck again and saw two black fins in the water which everyone took to be a shark. They kept disappearing and rising again, so Harry gave permission for one of the boats to be lowered to go in pursuit of him. The boat was soon full of volunteers as well as the crew, and the young ladies went too, but I had enough yesterday. Silva, one of the Quartermasters,

took the harpoon. It was most exciting watching the boat following the huge fish. At last down went the harpoon, the creature went up to the surface, just being touched, and it was found to be an enormous Sea Devil about 14 feet long, and surrounded by Pilot fish and suckers.

Being no doubt startled, down he went, as we feared, altogether but he re-appeared and this time the harpoon went right through him. The blood spouted up. Everyone on board was rushing about and shouting with excitement. They towed him along for a short time, then down he went again, tearing the harpoon right out of himself. It was a most wonderful and beautiful fish as we saw it gleaming and shining through the water, like some gigantic bird in shape. I wonder whether he received his death wound, or will live to enjoy himself again in his native element.

Several sharks have been seen around the ship, and albacore. A small shark caught this morning about three feet long.

Lat 1° 6' Long 21° 57' Distance 14 miles

March 27th
Still calm and intensely hot, we are still talking and thinking of the monster we saw yesterday and wishing it would reappear. I sat on deck all day with the exception of meals. In the evening we had a very good Minstrel Entertainment given by the midshipmen, 2nd, 3rd and 4th officers and one or two of the passengers. They sat in a circle on the main deck with black faces and dressed in white trousers and middies jackets, except Sam and Banjo who wore black trousers and white shirts with elaborate ties of scarlet, and Bones wore a wig, part of which stood on end every now and then.[6]

March 27th 1883
A sharp squall came on just before the conclusion accompanied by heavy rain. Everyone seized his or her chair and

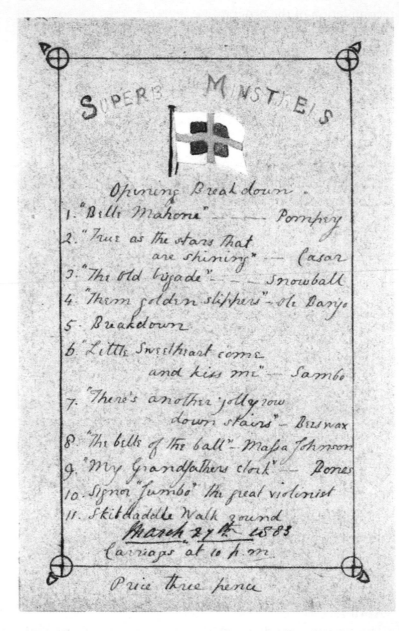

The Superb *Minstrels programme for 27 March 1883.*

decamped, but we were able to resume our places for the completion of the programme.

March 28th
Sighted and spoke with a large ship, the *Windsor Park* from London to Calcutta, 50 days out. A moderate breeze.
   Lat 2° 49' Long 23° 15'

March 29th
The *Windsor Park* still in company. A nice breeze, but the sun intensely hot. Sat on the poop till 11.30 finding the saloon too hot for cards.

March 30th
Breeze still freshening, and very welcome after the long calm we have had. Mersey brought his violin on deck in the evening, but somehow the dancing was not taken up with spirit and soon fell through.
   Lat 7° 35' Long 26° 4' Dist 171

March 31st
As strong breeze and head sea, causing some heavy pitching, under the effects of which a good many collapsed. I lay on the bed all day feeling wretched. Boxer came in to see me once or twice and seemed pretty lively. The dear old dog seems a link with home and brings so much to memory. It seems but the other day that he, Harold and Jesse were all playing on the hearthrug, babies together!
   A small charge was made for the admission the other night, and realized 16/-, half of which was put into the box in aid of the 'Merchant Seamen's Orphan Asylum' and the other for the 'Aged Seamen's Fund'.

April 1st
The sea has gone down during the night, and everyone has revived. I went on deck about 8 am till breakfast. Service at

10.30, a very small congregation feeling the heat, though the breeze is strong.

Heavy showers of rain during the day which drive us from the comfortable places we have taken on the poop. At the first possible moment we all come back like flies. Service in the saloon at 7.30. I played the hymns, and sat on deck till nearly bedtime.

April 2nd
As the ship is steadier and the weather fine, there are preparations going on for theatricals to come tomorrow evening. *Bombastes Furioso*[7] has been rehearsed for a week or two by four of the gentlemen. All morning I have been at work on a muslin cap for 'Dastafenia', making some braids of flax to represent hair and flowing curls. With the aid of a little rouge, my cotton dressing gown, an apron, mittens etc Mr Parkin was a very good 'get up'.

It is wonderful the resources one has to fly to on board ship for fancy dress. The king's crown was tin, decorated with little figures, a crimson shirt, white ducks, sea boots turned over with brown paper, and a ladies fur-lined cloak turned inside out made quite a regal-looking personage. The Prime Minister had a wig with a queue, knee breeches, low shoes with large pasteboard buckles. The coat trimmed with ruffles at neck and waist, also an imitation gold lace made out of rope, the effect of which was admirable. I made a bouquet of artificial flowers for a man to give a lady after the singing of 'For ever and for ever', which we had a strong suspicion was a burlesque on the young lady who practices [*sic*] so assiduously. We all enjoyed the play, which went off without a hitch, and was only too short.

Lat 17° 35' Long 29° 45' Distance 199.

April 4th
Our darling Jesse's 9th birthday. How I should like to kiss his bright little face! We can but pray for him and trust that

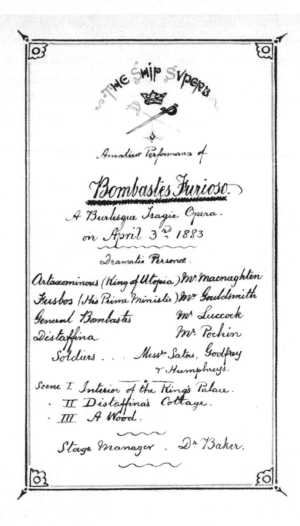

Programme for the performance of Bombastes Furioso

he is well and happy with dear Hal. It seems so long till we can meet again!

April 5th
A very fine day with a strong breeze. I knitted all morning. After dinner the steward favoured us with *Punch and Judy*.

The figures are made by himself, the dialogue was kept up very well between the Showman, who was invisible, and Mr Mann the 3rd officer whose face was decorated with a black eye, red nose and a beard of a few days growth! A shaky white hat with black band around it, a disreputable red handkerchief with the Pipes – and a drum slung over the shoulder – the hat was passed round afterwards and 12/- collected which was divided between the boxes.

Dist 109.

April 6th
A head wind and sea causing a great deal of pitching, I had to lie down most of the day! A homeward bound ship passed us, it was very tantalizing not to be able to send our letters.

Lat 27° 7' Long 29° 54' Dist 129

April 7th
Still feeling very squeamish, though the wind is more favourable, heavy pitching at times. Consoled myself with *Vanity Fair*. Boxer seemed to be out of sorts also, so I had him on the bed with me.

The *Windsor Park* still in company with us nearly a fortnight after we sighted each other.

Lat 30° 19' Long 30° Dist 192

April 8th Sunday
Service in the saloon 10.30. Mr Leacock played the piano as I still feel out of sorts, but the wind is now fair and the sea gone down a great deal.

Lat 33° 46' Long 28° 31' Dist 221

April 9th
Strong fair wind. Knitted all morning on deck and had the satisfaction of finishing Jesse's jersey. So much cooler that one appreciates a jacket or shawl. Only last week

we were sighing for cooler weather. After tea we played 'Nap' and *vingt et un* until 10 o'clock. We have a nice little party at our end of the table, and often a very merry one, weather permitting. A long sea voyage is an excellent test of character, and all weaknesses and peculiarities soon come to the surface. It is interesting to notice if one's first impressions are correct – I think all mine were, without exception.

Lat 37° 5' Long 26° 10' Dist 230

April 10th
A thoroughly wet day. We sat in the saloon all morning, some working, some reading, writing, copying music; draughts, chess and cards going on. Still a splendid fair wind and we have come 235 miles since midday yesterday.

April 13th
Our dear Harold's 11th birthday. I felt very sad at the thought that we are divided by so many miles. I trust he is well and happy. I indulged in a good cry before breakfast, which was a very foolish thing and gave me a headache for the rest of the day. I worked at his jersey, lay down in the afternoon, played *vingt et un* in the evening. Dist 226.

April 14th
Another birthday: my brother Oughton is 44 today. Poor old fellow, I wonder how he is! We, that is my three brothers and myself, are each divided by about the width of the globe.

Still a fair wind and we are rapidly nearing the Cape. Already many are speculating as to the probable time of arriving at Melbourne, though we have so many thousand miles yet to cross. Harry is delighted we are making such a good course, which makes up for the want of wind at the beginning of the voyage.

The ship rolled heavily at intervals yesterday, making meals a difficulty, as the dishes, glasses etc went sliding about, resulting in more than one breakage. Dressing is really hard work, staggering about one's cabin, and all things slipping and sliding out of reach!

After tea we had great fun over a game of 'Animal Grab', then a quiet rubber till 10 pm. We went on deck, there was a strong fair wind, but the decks were rather wet. Run today 143 miles.

April 15th Sunday
We are still going steadily along. Service at 10.30, Miss Bullions played for me. A very small congregation. I walked on deck till lunchtime. One or two albatross have been caught already. I cannot but feel sorry for the splendid birds, so helpless when one man seizes his beak, ties it firmly together, another secures his wings, another his legs, and the beautiful bright eyes turning rapidly from one to another. I hope he has not the pain of anticipating his fate. The death is generally a merciful one, by prussic acid, or a pin passed into the brain, which results in instant death. Then comes the skinning and the preserving, and the sportsman who has one of these magnificent specimens may well think himself fortunate.

Dist 262 miles

April 16th
A strong fair wind, and part of the day bright sun. I was so sleepy when the dressing bell rang at 8 am that Harry brought me my breakfast, so I did not make an appearance in the saloon much before 11, then worked at Harold's jersey until nearly dinner time. I finished *Vanity Fair* and played cards all evening. I did not go on deck, but everyone said it was a clear cold splendid night. The ship is almost as steady as a house, yet we are going about 12 knots an hour.

Lat 42° 1' Long 7° 8' Distance 217 miles

April 17th

Nearing the Cape rapidly. Every morning on waking I congratulate Harry and myself that our cabin is still dry, and we hope the new bulkhead will keep the water out all the way to Melbourne. It is really most unpleasant to have it wet as we had last voyage.

After breakfast I played two games of Cribbage with Mr Mann and won them as part of a tournament. I helped Harry copy out his log for about an hour. Began a pair of cuffs to be raffled in aid of the 'Box'.

Lat 42° 13' Long 12° 44' Dist 250.

18th April

A fine, pleasant day, with the ship very steady. The men gave an entertainment in the saloon, which was really enjoyable. They all sang their best, though of course one had to make allowance for pronunciation etc. Two of them Whitley and Stanton are very talented, the former as a comic singer and dancer, the latter as a Reciter; one piece was most amusing, *The One-legged Goose*. Programmes were sold for 2d each and realized 6/8 for the Life Boat Association.

Dist 125 miles

19th April

Wind fell light during the night, and not quite so favourable. During the day Miss Churnside and I made two pairs of warm cuffs to be raffled for the Orphan's Fund at 1d tickets, and the sum realised was 4/6, not as good as the price I got last year. We had a most amusing game after tea of 'Cross questions and Crooked Answers', also Consequences which were most laughable. A heavy swell on all day.

Lat 42° 31' Long 17° 56'

April 20th

Thick fog, rolling heavy sea, the dampness dripping from the rigging and sails. I tried to have a walk on deck after dinner,

Superb *Theatre of Varieties programme*.

but the ship was <u>jumping</u> about so much it was almost impossible, though a few struggled about and one or two fell, the deck being so slippery. Played Consequences and cards in the evening, the former caused a great deal of amusement.

Lat 43° 30' Long 21° 29' Dist 167

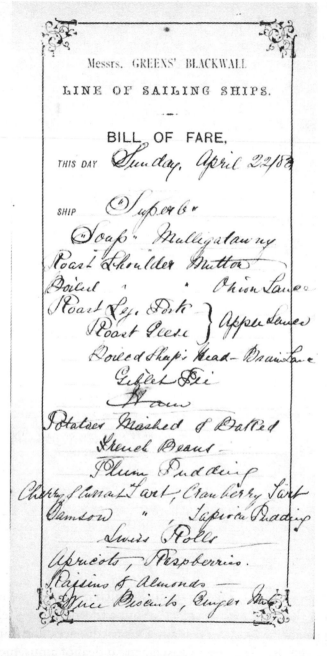

Menus for Sunday 22 April, 1883.

April 21st

Still the same unpleasant weather, thick fog, everything damp and uncomfortable. Mr Harvey, walking and running on a slippery deck, fell and unfortunately broke his wrist. He is a big man and I fear will feel the effects for a long time. Too complicated to venture on deck so knitted all afternoon. Consequences and Nap in the evening. Something in this weather makes me so sleepy that I have not heard the dressing bell for three mornings, and this morning there was a great scrimmage overhead, two dogs after a rat, all of which I slept through. So my dear old boy brought my breakfast at 9 o'clock, so I had only to eat it at my leisure before dressing.

April 22nd

Same wet, unpleasant weather, decks wet and slippery, another fall by which one of the sailors has broken a small bone in his hand. The time hangs rather heavily with the gentlemen who wander disconsolately up and down the saloon, now and then settling down to cribbage or Chess.

April 29th Sunday

A week has passed since the last entry in my diary, which has been passed in an anxious manner. Miss Bullions was taken seriously ill with an attack of spasms in the throat on Monday night about 11 o'clock. I went into the cabin just casually to wish the two girls goodnight, and while I was there the attack came on, and I went for the Doctor. It became so serious that he and I remained with her till 5 am on Tuesday morning, when Mrs Wells came to take my place and the Doctor went to lie down. Ever since, we have watched her every moment and at times it has been truly distressing to watch her struggle for breath and life with so little alleviation to give to the suffering.

Mrs Benson, Mrs Wells and I have taken it in turns day and night. At times it has been necessary for two to be in the cabin. Poor girl, she has borne it very patiently, and I am thankful to say she has rallied a little since yesterday. Illness and nursing are sufficiently distressing in a comfortable house and well appointed room, but in a ship's cabin, badly lighted, and rough weather, badly ventilated, everything you lay down has the risk of rolling away. Such necessary items as linseed poultice, chloroform, cups of beef tea, cold water, boiling water, tea spoons, fans, smelling salts, *sal volatile*,[8] all wanted in their turn, it requires some ingenuity to put them down out of hand so as to prevent a casualty, such as spilling water, soup etc. on the patient's bed, or even losing what may be the whole of a certain drug that may be on board. All this can only be realized by those who have experienced it.

Another sad case on board is that of Mr Andrews who has been and is suffering from a sort of melancholy depression. It is really wretched to see him wander about with his eyes looking frightened, and quite unable to fix his attention, apparently, even to answer the servants who attend on him at meal times.

The weather has been truly depressing, almost constant fog through the week, though we have made fair progress, being now just off the Crozet Islands.[9]

Dist 161 miles

May 1st
Thankful to say that though Miss Bullions has remained very ill since my last entry, she has now made a decided rallying point, want of sleep and appetite now being the chief difficulties.

Strong winds, and today we have had the sun, the first for three days. Last night we had some very heavy rolling. I was sitting up with Miss Bullions at about 1.30, when hearing a monotonous sound in the saloon as if a broom handle were rolling about, I rallied forth, candle in hand to stop it if possible. Arriving at the end of the saloon underneath the companion ladder, where it was very dark and my candle not much use, I was rather startled to see the

Superb alphabet

A stands for Australia to which we are bound
B is our Bosun whose pussy was drowned
C is our Captain, a man brave and true
D stands for doldrums which drenched us all through
E is the Engineer who makes silver rings
F is the Fo'c'sle where you hang out your things
G is the galley where presides Mr Fox
H is for H Lane jammed in a tin box
I for Ingram who wears baggy breeches
J stands for Jimmy who puts in the stitches
K is the Kelson which made but one fool
L was the Looby-one – Godfrey from school
M Mrs Matthews just entered the yoke
N is for Nelson who his finger did break
O is for Osburn who presides over the revel
P is for Plews the midshipmen's Devil
Q is the Quay from which we all started
R are the Relations from whom we are parted
S stands for the Sun Fish which Silva harpooned
T The theatricals in which Pochin was spooned
U's doggerel for Euchre which mademoiselle knows
V is Villard who swabs down her toes
W is Wilmot with his gingerly walk
X is a letter on which we can't talk
Y stands for Yule, you'll please note the pun
Z is the zig-zag course we have run.

figure of a man apparently on his hands and knees creeping about. It proved to be Mr Hardly-Wilmot, one of the
midshipmen on the same errand as I was. We both laughed
on recognition and he told me we were going at about 10
knots, which compensated for the miseries of the rolling.

I then went back to Miss Bullions and was in the middle of narrating my adventure, when the ship, giving an enormous lurch, sent me and the candle flying to the other side of the cabin and deposited me in sitting posture on the deck. The commotion woke up Miss Churnside who was sleeping in the other bunk. We all had a good laugh, my only anxiety being the lighted candle which however I had kept clutched firmly in my hand, so all was well. And I picked myself up, then the chair and we settled down until Mrs Wells came to relieve my watch at about 2.30 when I went to bed.

May 2nd
I spent the day as has been usual the last week, getting to bed about 2.30 am. I slept till 11. I found Miss Bullions going on pretty well. The weather is still thick and foggy.
    Lat 43° 25' Long 67° 58' Distance 257

May 3rd
A concert was fixed for this evening, as Miss Bullions is so much better, but unfortunately Mr Andrews has had a serious relapse, so it has been put off. We have a splendid fair wind. I finished Harold's jersey except one sleeve which must wait for wool until we get to Melbourne. Everyone is now feeling anxious to arrive in order to get letters and news of home. We might be off Cape Otway in a fortnight.
    Lat 43° 57' Long 71° 59' 177 miles

May 4th
Strong fair wind and sun shining. Miss Bullions quite convalescent, but poor Mr Andrews seriously ill, apparently unconscious. Daly is attending on him with frequent visits from the Doctor and the Steward.
    Lat 42° 57' Long 76° 28' Dist 198

May 5th
Strong, fair wind all the early part of the day, but lighter towards evening, sun shining in the afternoon. I worked at the flags for boys' jerseys till dinner. Afterwards I and two or three others repaired to the piano. Harry sang two songs, then Mr Warden played delightfully on the violin till tea time. I read till 8 pm when our usual party assembled with one consent for Loo at which we played till 10 pm. One young lady then came to me for permission to walk on deck for half an hour, I knew there was a special attraction, so consented, though I had to read her a little lecture on the proprieties, and suggested that 10 o'clock was late enough for a young lady in her teens to be walking with a gentleman friend when all the other ladies had retired. Fortunately she agreed with me at once.

Lat 42° 30' Long 82° 13' Distance 256

May 6th Sunday
Owing to the wind falling to light last night, we had a good deal of rolling which made sleep a difficulty. Harry brought me a cup of tea at 9 and I was only dressed just in time for Church at 10.30, after which everyone availed themselves of the lovely weather for a walk before lunch. Now I must turn to my home letters to have them ready for our arrival.

Dist 160 miles

May 7th
The best concert of the voyage took place last evening. The weather was so fine in the morning that it was decided on short notice. Everyone seemed in their best mood and the whole evening was a great success.

Lat 33° 46' Long 28° 39' Dist 221

Programme

Violin and piano	'Serenade'	*Gounod*
Song	'Far away from bonnie Scotland'	Miss Wells
Song	'Gallants of England'	Mr Blenkinsee
Song	'Shady O'Flynn'	Mrs Matthews
Song	'Isle of Beauty'	Captain Berridge
Recitation	'The Revenge'	Mr MacNaughton
Song	'Patrick Mind the Baby'	Mr Ingram
Recitation	'Tragic'	Mrs Matthews
Song	'Rose Marie'	Mr Fendelow
Song	'Parson and Clerk'	Mr Mann
Song	'Auntie'	Mrs Wells
Recitation	'Mr Squiggles Dinner'	Mr Laycock
Song	'Hunting Song'	Mr Pochin
Song	'The Whale'	Captain Berridge
Duet	'What are the Wild Waves Saying?'	Mrs Matthews and Mr Fendelow
	'God Save the Queen'	

May 8th

We woke this morning at 5 am with the rain pouring on the deck overhead and a <u>gale</u> blowing. Harry jumped and was arrayed in sea boots and oilskins in a very few minutes. The gale lasted all day, but being <u>fair</u>, we were consoled by the fact that it was helping us on our way. I went up the companion stairs once just to look at the big seas rolling up behind. After tea we played Loo till 10 o'clock. Poor Mr Andrews is no better, in fact weaker. I trust he may live to reach Melbourne.

Two of the passengers who <u>always</u> attend to their own wants at the dinner table before thinking of their neighbours. It was done one evening in an idle moment in the saloon by another passenger. Pencil drawing.

May 12th (Leicester Fair Day)
We have had three miserable days: rain, wind, pitching, rolling and everyone generally depressed.[10] Longing for the end of the voyage. Dressing in the morning is hard work, <u>everything</u> rolls away, and occasionally there is a smash in the way of a tumbler or jug or water bottle. Even the very water in the basin refuses to stay there, but flies out with an extra roll of the ship! Perhaps wetting the very garments one is just going to put on.

Poor Mr Andrews is getting weaker and weaker. One of the stewards slipped on the main deck yesterday and hurt his back. It is a mystery to me how the various dishes for the meals arrive safely through their <u>voyage</u> from the galley to the saloon! The main deck being constantly wet gets as slippery as ice.

Lat 29° 50' Long 11° 21' Dist 204

May 13th Sunday
We had a most horrid night, <u>rolling</u>, <u>pitching</u>, <u>lurching</u>. I had to leave the dinner table feeling queer and lay on the bed until it was time to <u>undress</u>. About 11 o'clock Miss Bullions came out of her cabin into the saloon for some water, a sudden lurch sent her all her length onto the cabin floor of Mr MacNaughton who was lying in bed probably half asleep. He roused up sufficiently to say, 'What's that row?' but the young lady had picked herself up and fled to her own cabin in confusion. Everyone weary and tired with the bad night, Harry more so than anyone, so there was no service this morning. I did not come into the saloon much before lunch, feeling very shaky, regaled myself with a biscuit. We are much steadier now at 2 pm and longing to get past Cape Leeuwin the extreme point of Western Australia, when there is hope of a more regular sea.

Lat 39° 23' Long 111° 32' Dist 218

May 14th
Poor Mr Andrews died at midnight, and was buried at 8 am. Harry read the service and most of the gentlemen attended, and all the crew and officers. A funeral at sea is very solemn and impressive. We are all so well-known to each other. It will be sad news for the poor wife and little children at home.

Lat 39° 15' Long 116° 34' Dist 235

May 15th
We have been <u>flying</u> through the water the last twenty-four hours and though all expected a good run it was an agreeable surprise to hear we had done 302 miles.

'Lines on the voyage' [some of it written
in a different hand]

… Tis thirteen weeks or rather more
Since England's coast, our native shore
We left, for Melbourne bound
And though we've struggled might and main
Australia's sunny clime to gain
We haven't got there yet!
Of course they say, 'We're almost there'
'Our days on board will be few'
But 'There's many a slip 'twixt cup and lip'
Is a saying old and true.
For a good head wind, or none at all
Or a heavy gale, or a sudden squall
Might lengthen our trip, or disable our ship
Or prevent us arriving at all!
Put away such gloomy thoughts as these
There's much that will sadden, but more that will please
So let's take life's sunny side.
And now for a yarn of our ship *Superb*.'

[In different handwriting]
As there's little to tell perhaps 'twill be as well
To attempt that little in Rhyme
For the first few weeks we walked the deck
From morn till late at night,
And we looked at the water, and looked at the sky,
When land was no longer in sight.
We talked, 'tis true, of what we'd do
But at last there came a day when a concert was held in
    the large saloon
To pass the time away.

'Tis March the fourth and Sunday morn.
A bright and lovely day
Like a cloud rising from the sea

The isle Madeira lay.
Then Palma, Ferro, Teneriffe
All in due course we past,
And twenty-four the tropics beat
Though late, we're crossed at last.

And now we hope our luck may change
For hoping can't do harm
For up to now we've had our share
Of want of wind, or calm!
But now a warm and steady breeze
Fills the once flapping sail,
And all on board are bright and gay
To see the favouring gale
On Monday the twelfth at seven o'clock.
In the evening the dead horse was sold;
A custom that's now rather gone out of date
And its origin wonderfully old,
When the bidding has ceased,
And no money is called,
The horse and his man
To the Yard Arm must shift
A blue light is burnt
And his horse cut adrift.
On the fourteenth of March
In the evening at eight
A fancy dress ball
By the help of the mate
Was got up, but the sea made it awkward to stand
For those accustomed to walking on land.
The costumes were equal to any ashore.
We danced through the programme
And then wished for more.
Thus came to an end our fancy Dress Ball
To be talked of for days and remembered by all.
And now for a time we did nothing but play
Quoits, Cricket, and cards all everyday

And we lounged and we slept
And we talked and we smoked
And for Neptune's arrival all earnestly hoped.
And prayed that a breeze
Might waft us away
To the Father's Domain
Where Neptune holds sway.

At last we've almost reached the line
And all are keen to view
And some to feel, King Neptune's power
And wonder what he'll do.
His secretary's come on board
And given each a letter
And will on board tomorrow come
At tea but now must go
As he has notes for other ships
Before he goes below
'Good night' says he, 'Goodnight' say we
He hails his boat afar
A boat is seen, behold it is
A lighted tub of tar.
Next morn will be a busy one
So up my boys with the rising sun
Begin the work, let's get it done
Ere Neptune comes to start the fun.

The bath is rigged, the pumps are worked
And soon begins the fill
And all are getting something done
And working with a will
To attempt to describe the whole scene from the first
And who was let off, and who was ducked worst
Would take too much time, so I'll just say
That we all shall remember that wonderful day.
First the Doctor was asked if he thought you were ill
And whether or not prescribed you a pill

Henry Berridge as a baby.

Henry Berridge as a
young boy.

Maud as a baby with her brother William Henry Timperley.

Maud as a young girl with her brothers William and Frank.

Henry Berridge in 1864.

Maud Timperley and Henry Berridge's engagement photo, 1868.

Maud and crew on board the *Walmer Castle* in 1869. Henry is just behind her.

The *Walmer Castle* in dock. Note the square windows, similar to those on the *Superb*.

Henry (centre) and his crew on *Highflyer* in 1874.

The *Highflyer*.

The *Superb* crew in 1883.

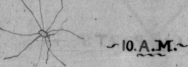

~ 10. A. M. ~

Neptune will hold a levee to which all who have not been presented to his Majesty before, will be required to present themselves and go through ye usual ceremonies.

An invitation by Neptune for the 'Crossing the Line' ceremony on board the *Superb* in 1883.

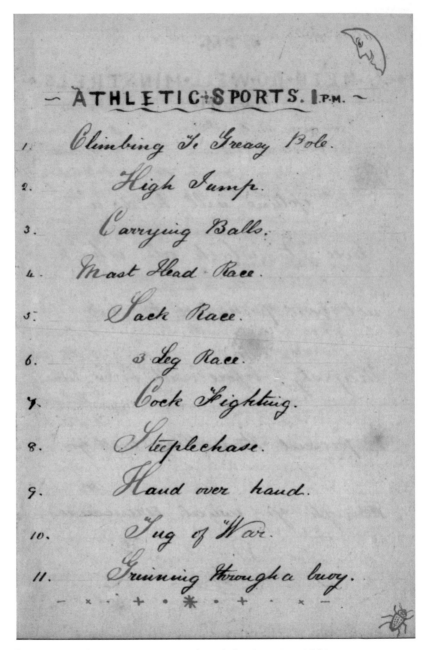

~ ATHLETIC SPORTS. 1 P.M. ~

1. Climbing Ye Greasy Pole.
2. High Jump.
3. Carrying Balls.
4. Mast Head Race.
5. Sack Race.
6. 3 Leg Race.
7. Cock Fighting.
8. Steeplechase.
9. Hand over hand.
10. Tug of War.
11. Running through a buoy.

Programme for a sports event on board the *Superb* in 1883.

• Y.P.M •

• Yᴇ • NE'ER • DO • WELL • MINSTRELS •

1.	Chorus	Troupe
2.	"Those girls at the School" .	A. G. Plews.
3.	"The slave's Dream".	A. G. Golding
4.	"Will you love me when I'm old".	C. Whiteley
5.	"By the Blue Alsatian Mountains".	W. Coxen.
6.	"Gum Tree Canoe".	D. Mersey.
7.	"Recitation".	H. Stanton
8	Step Dance.	C. Whiteley
	Interval of Ten Minutes.	
9.	"I wu'it have old Ireland run down".	W. Pulse
10.	"Stick to your mother Tom".	J. Spoorn
11.	"Slatty Hells."	H. Stanton
12.	"The Old Folks at Home".	A. Golding
13.	"Slavery days".	C. Whiteley
14.	Recitation.	H. Stanton
15.	Step dance.	R. Densley
16	"Skipper and his boy."	R. Bailei
17.	"Bye and bye". (Duet)	A Plews & C. Whi
18	"The men of merry England".	P. Nelson

God save the Queen.

Programme for the Ne'er Do Well Minstrels on board the *Superb* in
1883.

The *Superb* docked at Sandgate Railway Pier, Melbourne. Image held at the State Library, Victoria.

The crew of *Superb*, possibly in 1883.

Cliff House in San Francisco in the 1880s.

Trialling the lifeboat system at Cliff House.

Unloading coal from ships at Howard Street dock, 1898.
Courtesy of Online Archive of California, University of California, Berkeley.
Roy D Graves Pictorial Collection.

Boxer, photographed in Melbourne 1883. No date is given for his death.

Maud and Henry in later life.

Maud, Harold and Jesse
after Henry's death.

Jesse Berridge and his first
wife Edna

Jesse later in life.

Harold Berridge and his first wife Alice.

Harold later in life.

Left: Maud's brother W H Timperley as a young sub-inspector in the Western Australia Police Force.

Below: His wife Rebecca Timperley.

Then the Barber, the part that we most of us feared
With his wonderful razor cut everyone's beard
And that being over we backward were chucked
But four bears in the bath each and all to be ducked
And the Concert followed this
Most wonderful display
Then someone said, 'Why, happy thought
Let's try and do a play'.
We chose the piece <u>Bombastes</u>
And in a week or so
The Bill was posted up to say
'*Bombastes Furioso*
For the first time on board this ship
Tomorrow after tea
On the Poop Deck will be performed
Programmes and places free.'
The King and brave Bombastes
Do Distaffina court
The audience shout their loud applause
But say the play's too short
And hope we'll give another one
Before the weather's rough
Or give them two if there isn't one
That will be long enough.

Farewell! Farewell! fine weather
Adieu ye sunny sky
For the wind is blowing fiercely
And the sea is running high
And flying along with a steady breeze
She rises merrily
Over each wave that would check her course
As she breasts the foaming sea.
And thus for some weeks we went along
Till one day our captain said,
'I fear we shall lose e're very long
This glorious South East trade.'

His words came true in a day or two
Our jovial Captain's right
For all on board can clearly see
The wind is falling light.
And then there came an awful time
The wind now here, now there
And first we braced the yards close up
And then we hauled them square
To keep our good ship on her course
The sailors trim the sail
And when it's done it's ten to one
The wind is sure to fail.
Then from another quarter comes. So pull with might
    and main
That's right my hearties – the wind
It's shifted round again. At length we made another start
And pleasantly were sailing
We've left the calms and are bowling along
With a westerly wind prevailing.
And around the ship the Albatross
The pigeon from the Cape
The Mollyhawk and other birds
Of various hue and shape
Are whooping, screeching, fighting
As their downward course they take
To seize the food thrown overboard
And floating in our wake.
And now the cunning fisherman
Behind the wheel, with coiled line
And baited hook in hand
The bait is thrown, the line runs out
The birds set up a cry
But e'er their swoop, the coils paid out
Let's have another try
For several times they would not take
That little bit of bait

But hovered round suspiciously
Until it was too late.
The fisherman he called aloud
And used a naughty word
'...–,' says he, 'if you and me
Don't catch that – bird'
Says he, 'I've often heard it said, and it may be true perhaps
That they will take the baited hook
When mixed with other scraps.
But where to get those scraps,' says he.
'Why bless it that's the rub.'
He gives the worthy butcher grog
The butcher gives him grub
Over the stern a floating mass…

May 16th

Still a strong fair wind, all through the night we have been going ten and eleven knots so were not surprised at the run, 266 miles.

Everyone is in good spirits at getting so near to Melbourne. This evening we had a capital entertainment; two plays called *Cut off with a shilling* and *Taming a tiger*. The acting was admirable, especially that of Mr Pochin as Mrs Gathorne, and the Doctor as Col Bemers. The stage was at the foot of the companion ladder, with a background of flags the effect was very good and it was truly amusing to see Mr Pochin acting the part of a pretty coquettish <u>bride</u> flirting with her husband who was Mr MacNaughton in an exquisite morning suit and flower in his buttonhole.

Between the pieces we had a very nice duet (piano and violin) between Miss Bullions and Mr Warden, encored, then followed by two songs from Mr Fendelow, 'True to the last' and 'Village Blacksmith'. We all enjoyed the evening thoroughly.

At 10.30 I went to my neighbour's cabin and felt it my duty to give Lily a little lecture on the subject of her walking and talking so much with Mr Hall, as she is placed under our charge for the voyage, one is in rather a predicament between not wishing to interfere with her enjoyment, and allowing her to be perhaps drawn into any position her father might object to.

May 18th
The Auction last night was great fun, all the articles for sale were placed on the saloon table for inspection. At 7.30 Mr Golding and Mr Mann were 'got up' as auctioneer and Clerk. The former made a witty little opening speech to the effect that, the previous evening we had witnessed *Cut off with a shilling*, but they hoped to cut off with a great many shillings. We had also seen *Taming a tiger*, but a more wonderful process was to be gone through, viz: raising the wind. There was some spirited bidding. I secured a hot water plate, a leather watch guard and two packets of 'Good Words' and 'Argosy'.

May 19th
We are all speculating as to the probability of sighting Cape Otway tonight. So far the wind is favourable. We can do nothing but talk of how many miles it is, and how many miles an hour we can do, have done, will do, through all the morning.

After tea we sat down to Loo, a little after ten Mr Barker reported <u>Land</u> on the Port bow! We all rushed on deck at once, to see what looked like a cloud, but we were only too delighted to believe it was land!

Cape Otway was sighted soon after from the mast head, and about 12 was visible from the deck. Everyone was walking and talking and thoroughly excited. I believe the general inclination was to shake hands all round. I made some coffee for Mr Barker, Mr Vale, Mr Mason, Mrs Wells, Harry, Miss

Bullions and myself. About 1 o'clock I went to bed and slept delightfully.

May 20th Sunday
When I woke this morning at 7, the 'dead lights' were open, the first time for weeks and we had the pleasure of seeing the land quite distinctly, and occasionally when there was a bright gleam of sunshine, it looked very pretty – as indeed any land would do after fourteen weeks of sky and water. Now all our thoughts are bent on receiving letters and news of home.

We are going along splendidly and hope to be through the heads this afternoon, and the Pilot Cutter is in sight.

11.54 am the Pilot came on board. We passed through the heads about 2 o'clock. The rain at intervals drove us down below, which rather spoilt the pleasure of approaching land. In the afternoon about 5 o'clock, to everyone's disappointment it fell a dead calm. We were very near the land and found a good deal to interest us in watching the breakers on the rocks, the variety of light and shade. All hope was given up of reaching the pier tonight, so we have to summon as much patience as possible to our aid, to wait for tomorrow morning.

May 21st
It was truly delightful to find ourselves within half a mile of the pier, to watch the various boats approach the ship from the shore, above all, the one which brought the shipping clerk with our letters. We watched him climb the ship's side, and could hardly wait with propriety while he shook hands with Harry and the officers, welcoming the ship into port once more.

We followed him downstairs into the saloon, and it must have been rather ludicrous if we had noticed ourselves, a party of 30 or 40 grown-up people following each other like a game of 'Follow the Leader'. The letters were soon given out, and each individual deep in perusal. We had the happiness of knowing that our dear ones at home, especially our children, were well. The next thing to do was to add a postscript to the fourteen letters I had already written, and then Mrs Benson, Mrs and Miss Wells and I scrambled down a rope ladder into a small boat, to take our letters to the Post, as the English mail was leaving the next day.

On our return to the pier we found the *Superb* alongside, and our voyage was really over.

May 24th
Having decided to come and live on shore for a time, we took up our quarters at the St Kilda Coffee Palace[11] today, and I think we shall be very comfortable.

Being the Queen's birthday, a review was held in Albert Park, also races at Flemington. We had tickets given us for the latter, and took Miss Bullions with us. The weather was not very genial, but the change was delightful from life on board. Miss Bullions and I did our share of quizzing the Ladies costumes, and the Gentlemen's too, for that matter! Mr Barker was there, looking supremely happy with his fiancée. Coppertop looked rather desolate walking about alone. Mr Vale was there also and took charge of Miss Bullions as she wanted to leave before the last race.

We arrived at the hotel as the dressing bell rang and at 6 o'clock sat down to *Table d'Hote* which was plainly but well served. After dinner, Harry went to the Smoke Room and I adjourned to the Drawing Room with some curiosity as to the occupiers! A lady and her daughter were at some knitting so I took up a book. Presently two young men came in, all in the room had travelled a good deal so the conversation soon became very animated comparing England with the Colonies; 'Frisco with China, Japan, India etc., and as the lady (who proved to be the widow of a large squatter[12]) had been everywhere but Japan, even through 'Thieves Theatre' in London, was a very great talker and gave her experiences without reserve, we had a good deal to amuse and interest us!

There is so little stiffness out in Australia compared to England. In some ways it is agreeable, but classes are so mixed up that every now and then one gets a shock!

May 25th

Very pleasant to wake up this morning and find myself in a <u>bedroom</u>. We went down to breakfast about 9 o'clock, and had some delicious fish, coffee, fresh bread and butter.

After breakfast Harry went to the ship, and I did a little unpacking, previous to going to town for shopping, which is a most agreeable pastime after the long voyage.

In the evening we went to the theatre to see a play called *Naked Truth*, which was horrid though there was some good acting in it. Got back to the hotel about 12 o'clock.

May 26th

Called on Mr and Mrs Benson who are staying at the Prince of Wales Hotel at St Kilda. It is a pretty house standing back from the road, with a verandah running round and nearly hidden by large Australian shrubs such as Morton Bay figs and wattle. Football match in the afternoon.

May 27th Sunday

A lovely bright morning with a soft balmy breeze. We walked to church in St Kilda, towards the esplanade, the sea was sparkling, and we could see the ships lying along the two piers at Sandridge. A nice quiet little service and an excellent sermon. Coming out we overtook Mrs Benson, and also Mr Pratt who came over with us last year, and enjoyed the walk back to the hotel. After dinner we walked to Mr Ellery's house about two miles. The air was delicious, and had it not been for the <u>mud</u> we should have had a pleasant walk. Tea at 6, and some chit chat till about 9, when we started through the Domain, part of the Government reserve, to the St Kilda road for the returning bus.

May 28th
We dined at Mr Coles after having spent the afternoon on board. A great deal of rain and wind.

May 31st
Went to a concert at the Town Hall for the benefit of Max Vogrich [an Austrian pianist and composer]. The hall looked extremely pretty, nearly everyone being in full dress. The music was not particularly enjoyable, the performance on the piano being to my mind more <u>wonderful</u> than pleasing, though Vogrich must be very popular here as a wreath was thrown to him and afterwards two bouquets. One enormous bouquet was handed onto the platform by a little child.

      After the concert we went for a feast of <u>oysters</u> at Heard's before the train left for St Kilda. Bye the bye, I did enjoy one part of the concert, that was the singing of part songs by the members (gentlemen) of the Melbourne 'Liederstafel', which was delightful.

June 2nd
Having tickets given us for some trotting races at the Elsternwick Course, we went there, but the rain came down incessantly which seemed to damp the spirits of the proceedings, in more senses than one. The races were very poor, and we were not sorry when it was time to leave. Having found the running car we had engaged to take us back to the station, we found the driver decidedly <u>elated</u>, also the gentleman who shared it with us. They had some altercation, which resulted in the cabman driving us as recklessly as possible, narrowly escaping the other vehicles, and sending showers of mud all round. I was relieved when we drew up at the station and we could jump out, even though it was very nearly into a broad flowing gutter which we strongly suspected the cabman intended us to get into! If so, he was

disappointed, for we managed to jump <u>over</u>, but really gutters in and around Melbourne are not trifles. People have been drowned in them, and a false step might at any time result in a thorough drenching.

June 3rd

We are much disappointed at learning that instead of going straight to England the ship is chartered to go to Newcastle NSW for coal, thence to San Francisco. We are to sail next week probably, so our time in Melbourne this year will be short.

We did not go to church this morning, as I did not feel very well, so Harry wrote letters for the English Mail which leaves tomorrow.

In the afternoon we walked over to Hawthorne, or should I say we went most of the way by train, and walked the remainder. The Stackpooles live in a pretty Australian house, built on the ground floor only with a broad verandah running around. Two of the boys were looking out for us at the gate, as we walked up the drive they gathered me a red rose and some mignonette. Indeed, it is difficult to realise this is midwinter!

We sat in the drawing room for a time, talking to little Kitty, Val and Zoe. About two years ago our own darlings visited the Stackpooles with us, and whenever I go there I like to fancy I see them running in the garden with the others, but it makes me sad to think how very far away we are! Though I feel it is better for them to be in England than here!

Leaving at about 8 o'clock the children gave me a little white kitten which Mrs Cox has taken charge of until we sail.

June 4th

This afternoon I called on Mrs Ashurst and Mrs Godfrey and arrived at the Walshes where we were engaged to dine about 5.30, Harry coming in a little later. We had some very nice music and one or two dances, then Mr Clark walked back with us to St Kilda. It was a delicious balmy evening, though showery, and we arrived back at the Coffee Palace about 11.30.

June 5th
Our talkative friend Mrs Tuson and her daughter have left the hotel for Sydney, also another lady, so the Drawing Room seems very quiet now. Last Saturday night we went to the Bijou Theatre and thoroughly enjoyed *Diplomacy*. It was acted for 1800 nights in London, and was better done here than most things are. It is a dear little theatre, and thoroughly comfortable.

June 14th
We have said good-bye to St Kilda and brought all our belongings on board again. We came in time for lunch. Afterwards I unpacked and set the cabin straight. We dined at the Bijou Restaurant then went to hear Dr Simms [*sic*] lecture on Physiognomy, which was rather interesting, then to Heard's for a last supper of oysters for the present. Just missed the 10.20 train to Sandridge so had to wait an hour. On arrival at the pier we found Tibb's boat awaiting us, also two clerks from the shipping office and about half a dozen midshipmen. We took our places, the water was smooth and with a fair wind we had a pleasant sail across the bay to the ship. We scrambled up the ladder and once more began life on board ship. I went into our cabin and 'turned in', and I must say I found the bed extremely hard! The white kitten was comfortably curled up at the foot and remained there all night.

June 15th
A most delicious morning, smooth water and bright sunshine. There is a most extraordinary stillness and quiet prevails over the ship. Harry was obliged to go once more on shore, but returned in the middle of the day about 1.00

when we weighed anchor and sailed away as though we had been a yacht!

June 16th

Passed through Port Phillip heads late last night then Mr Beede the pilot left us. Another Pilot is on board to take us around the coast.

All this morning we have been sailing along splendidly, close to a bold rocky coast and through many islands, one named Rodondo was remarkable, rising sheer out of the water with a number of large trees to the summit about 500 feet high.

June 19th

Ever since we left Melbourne the weather has been perfect, soft, balmy and delicious. The wind fell light for a time and we were almost becalmed, but today it has freshened and we are now off Cape Jervis, and this morning we can see the lighthouse, or rather the light. The ship seems so strange with only one passenger besides myself. It is like an enchanted ship where everyone is under a spell and waiting for someone to break it!

June 20th

A most exquisite Australian winter's day: brilliant sunshine, the air soft yet exhilarating! As Mr Barker remarked, 'Life is worth living on a day like this'.

We are gently sailing along the coast, sometimes almost becalmed, then a little breeze springs up. The line of the coast seems to change little, here and there in a hollow we see the smoke of wood fires rising, which shows that a family or two may be living there. I cannot imagine what such an existence must be without any further interest or excitement than minding sheep or cattle, cutting wood and drawing water with almost perpetual fine weather.

I sat on deck knitting all morning, dinner at 1.30, read on deck till 4, then I came down to the cabin to rest my eyes from the glare of the sun on the water. Tea at 6. I played the piano and tried some songs, and Harry too, for about an hour, then we went on deck and sat in the lovely moonlight and starlight, but there was no breeze which disappointed Harry, but I found it too pleasant to wish for anything different.

June 21st
A change in the weather, the sky is overcast, and heavy clouds seem to be gathering on the horizon. I went on deck at 1/2 past 8 and the first news I heard was that the tug was seen coming to fetch us in. It produced an excitement at once, everyone watching the little *Leo* as she advanced, but the Pilot said she was too small and not powerful enough, so she had to turn back, then came the *Bungaree* which was accepted and soon made fast. We are now in tow and proceeding at a pretty good speed towards Newcastle.

June 22nd
We arrived at Newcastle yesterday and judging from the appearance of the town from the water it is not so ugly as has been represented to us. Built on the side of a hill, it has rather a picturesque appearance. Just at the entrance to the river, there is Signal Hill, and beyond a lighthouse built on a high rock which stands by itself almost, and to which the name 'Nobby's' seems very appropriate. There are a great number of large ships and steamers lying at anchor, and also alongside the pier waiting for the coal. There would be a very heavy sea breaking here in rough weather but for the breakwater, which has been built out of enormous stones, some weighing 15 or 20 tons.

This evening Harry and I were on deck sitting in the moonlight. The air is delicious, water quite calm. The lights of the town twinkling on the hillside look very pretty, and a small steamer ferry rushing up and down and across the river, gives some animation to the scene.

One of the most amusing things that happened on our arrival was to see the number of <u>Butchers</u> that besieged the ship, soliciting orders. Of course only <u>one</u> could be patronized, the rest went off in the sulks, and grumbling as though they had been <u>asked</u> to come on board and present their various cards.

June 23rd

I paid my first visit on shore at Newcastle and found that certainly 'distance lends enchantment' in some cases. There is one long principle street running the length of the town, the railway and the wharves being on one side and short streets running up the steep hillside on the other. Some of them are decent, others are very dirty and rough. Tumbledown wooden cottages, and large stones thrown down the centre of the road. Having climbed to the top of one of the better ones, we found ourselves near Christ Church Cathedral. It is a very primitive building, and now being pulled down for the new cathedral to be built, as the <u>site</u> is a splendid one and commands a magnificent view of the mouth of the Hunter River, Signal Hill, Nobby's Lighthouse, islands, the shipping breakwater, and all the outskirts of the town below, as well as a fine stretch of open sea.

The row of about a mile in our own boat from the wharf to the ship was very pleasant. Mr Mackenzie is now 3rd officer, Mr Carter, Mr Hills, Mr Simms, Mr Hurrell, Mr Hardley-Wilmot formed the boat's crew. Climbing up the ship's ladder required some energy and <u>tact</u>, as she is now very light and high out of the water.

June 27th

Today we availed ourselves of the kind offer of Mr Thomson (the Butcher) to lend us a buggy and horse, he moreover let his son go with us on horseback, as Pilot. When we started off our party was highly suggestive of John Gilpin's. Mr Golding and Harry were in the front

seat, Mackenzie and I behind. Our horse was a most energetic piebald who objected to a whip strongly, but he went
splendidly when there was no occasion to use one. For the
first few miles the road was very ugly: flat with occasional
patches of sand and scrub, then it improved, fine gum
trees with here and there land under cultivation, looking
delightfully lush and green especially the Indian corn,
after the scrub which has a most depressing appearance.
We saw a Chinaman busily watering his garden with two
large watering cans suspended from a yoke on his shoulder, so he had only to walk along and guide the rose of the
can. A much less troublesome proceeding than <u>carrying</u>
one can at a time. Certainly 'John' knows a great many
things!

The object of our drive was to see an orange garden. We
soon arrived at 'Waratah', the owner very kindly showed us
round and gave us a quantity of fruit, also passion fruit which
I thought delicious. He was rather an original, answering all
our questions <u>very</u> deliberately and apparently summing us
up in his mind, and I think favourably at last. He told us
he was a <u>German</u>, and had come out to the colony in 1838.
The orange trees were very fine ones and nearly covered with
fruit. After walking home and admiring everything, even the
pumpkins and guavas, he took us into a large shed where
there were immense casks of wine of his own making, with
the old-fashioned wine presses standing around. Of course,
at this time of year, the vines are bare and pruned ready for
the next season, coming into leaf about October. We enjoyed
sitting in the shade, and made an excellent lunch of sand-
wiches, oranges and colonial wine, which our entertainer
drew off the cask into tumblers. Then, being rested and
having thoroughly enjoyed our trip into the country, we bid
them adieu and took our places again in the buggy. On our
return, one escort took us to see the 'Crystal Palace' gardens,
which was partly a tea garden, and partly a menagerie. We
strolled about looking at the birds and animals, and again

took our places in the buggy, reaching Newcastle after about an hour's drive, having had a most enjoyable afternoon.

July 1st Sunday

Harry and I went ashore this morning in the boat, it was rather stormy and cold. We attended service at Christ Church and remained for Holy Communion, the first time we have been able to do so since leaving England. It was a quiet and reverent service. From the churchyard there is a magnificent view of the mouth of the Hunter River, all the shipping lying at anchor, Nobby's and Signal Hill in the distance. Walking down to the wharf we found the boat awaiting us and reached the ship in time for dinner at 1.30. I sat on deck in the afternoon watching the boats and ferries going up and down. Wrote letters most of the evening.

July 3rd

We have renewed our acquaintance with Mr and Mrs Shaw living here, with whom we had such a pleasant day at Parramatta NSW last year. We took tea with them today and have all decided to go to the Newcastle Rowing Club Ball. It will be something to do, but of course knowing no one here, it will be rather tame for us.

July 4th

I went to the dressmakers about having my black silk <u>titivated</u> for the Ball, and succeeded in getting two lovely sprays of crimson poppies to trim it.

July 6th

The Ball came off last night – and must have been a great success. Everyone seemed to know everyone, the music was good, also the floor, and decorations extremely pretty consisting of flags, evergreens and oars and an outrigger suspended from the ceiling. Some of the fancy dresses were very pretty, but some very tawdry. A Puritan maid Ebony, Beppo is 'La

Mascotte', a courtier at the time of Charles were amongst the best, also Alegria. Of course we felt a little out in the cold, knowing only a very few. Still, it was amusing to look on, and there was a very nice supper spread in a lower room. We left about 3 am and Mr and Mrs Shaw kindly gave us a bed – we slept till 11.30 – then we got up and after a cup of tea proceeded on board. In the afternoon I had a very bad headache, owing I suppose to the musical excitement and late hours.

July 7th
In the afternoon we walked to the football ground to watch a match. There were a few people there, some nice-looking girls dressed with very good taste. Most of the Newcastle team are very big young men and look as strong as possible, the distinctive colours were red and blue, the former being Newcastle, the latter Sydney.

July 8th
Sunday morning: Harry and I went ashore in the boat for church. It was a most lovely morning, and a quiet placid feeling around us, like Sunday morning. The church is on the top of a hill and we had a pretty good climb. Mr and Mrs Shaw, their two little girls (Amanda and Corinda!) and Mr Scott came back to dinner with us.

July 9th
A strong wind blowing from the land. The ship lying over and I suppose bobbing about as I have had a bad headache all day.

July 10th
Mr Barker arrived back this morning after his holiday in Melbourne. We intend starting for Sydney on Wednesday.

July 12th
Our visit to Sydney put off till tomorrow. In the morning I wrote to my darling Harold. After dinner went ashore with

Harry, while he transacted business at the office, I strolled on the beach, taking Boxer with me, and watched the magnificent breakers come rolling in. This is a fine coast, very bold, but terrible for any poor ship to come too near. The roar of the breakers this afternoon was like artillery. Harry came to meet me, and after resting on the cliff for a time, we walked back to the wharf where the boat awaited us and arrived on board about 5.00.

July 14th

We went on board the *Maitland*[13] at 10 pm and walked about deck till 11, which was the time fixed for starting. Mr Barker and Mr Golding came on shore with us, we went to see the Shaws for an hour before coming on board. It seems so strange starting off on a paddle steamer. I have never been in one since my journeys from the Isle of Man to Liverpool when I was a girl, and suffered indescribable miseries from seasickness. Now I am an old sailor.

We left the wharf punctually at 11. There was the usual bell ringing and commotion, then with a puff of steam and smoke we glided off but the water was so smooth and the boat so steady that one might imagine the shore was receding into space instead of the steamer going on her way!

We watched 'Nobby's' almost out of sight, then, while Harry had a last pipe I went to our cabin – which was the tiniest I have ever been in. With all my practice in climbing up the ship's ladder lately, my capabilities were put to the test when I attempted to get into bed! However I accomplished it and could not help laughing at the elevated position. But the two little bunks were most comfortable. In the middle of the night we heard the most appalling groans and screams from the next cabin. While only half awake I heard a most sympathetic voice say, 'Wake up, old man, wake up!' and as everything was soon quiet we came to the conclusion that someone was suffering from nightmare!

The *Maitland* was alongside the Sydney wharf about 5 am this morning, but we did not care to 'turn out' until about 8, when we took a Hansom and came to Petty's Hotel.[14]

The air was so fresh and sweet, the sun shining, and Petty's looked like an old friend. We were in time for breakfast, which we thoroughly enjoyed, then strolled into the town, which seemed specially attractive after Newcastle. Mr Lockwood asked us to meet in the afternoon to go to Manly Beach. We took the small steamer at 2 o'clock, and certainly the bay is most enchanting, fresh views opening out on either side every few minutes. At Manly we climbed a small rocky hill at the top of which was a large stone kangaroo roughly carved. Of course the view all round was exquisite, the open ocean on one side, the Island harbour on the other, the sunshine, and <u>perfectly</u> clear air is most delicious!

We got back to the hotel just in time for dinner at 6. We were both tired, so rested on the verandah,[15] which is a very favourite resort: some of the gentlemen smoking, the ladies lounging in their pretty dresses, the moon shining and presently a harp and violin were played in the street opposite. Went to bed at 10.

July 15th Sunday
Went to church, then went by steamer across to Milson's Point where we found Mr Lockwood awaiting us to take us to dinner. After dinner we strolled down to the water's edge. The country here is the most extraordinary combination of rock and vegetation, trees and shrubs growing down to the very edge of the sea, and great barren rocks suddenly rising out of the most lovely garden, or in the middle of a public street! Crossed the bay, returning by moonlight. Sat on the verandah till 11 pm chatting with the Bowes who had been to see some orange growers, the crop of one had been sold for £3,000 and the other for £5,000. It seems extraordinary but the mass of fruit is magnificent.

July 16th

Had a walk through the town and took my fill of shop-gazing, then I had my hair cut by a talkative Frenchman. About 4 o'clock in the afternoon we started down to the wharf, as Captain Kidler invited us to dine on board the *Cuzco*.[16] We found the little steam launch awaiting us and were soon gliding through the water on our way to the *Cuzco*. In about 20 minutes we arrived. The captain received us at the gangway and we strolled about the beautiful deck, looked at the saloons, had a peep at the engines, which Captain Kidler calls his three thousand horses. Then came dinner. I was the only lady, there were besides ourselves the three officers, purser and chief engineer. A great deal of cheerful chat went on through dinner, most of which I could appreciate as it related to a voyage in the *Walmer Castle* to Melbourne thirteen years ago [1870], when Harry and I were first married and Captain Kidler was then second officer.

After dinner he took us in the steam launch, a lovely little trip to Mosman's Bay. The moon was shining brightly and the air was soft and delicious. We returned to shore about 9 o'clock, the red and green lights of the ships and the light of the town glimmering on the water, with brilliant electric light from the South Head Lighthouse, with the outline of the shore varying every moment, made a most beautiful picture.

July 17th

Today we paid a visit to the Chinese quarter, and Harry gave me a lovely China tea set. It is quite an entertainment to have a conversation with 'John Chinaman'. Mrs Lockwood came in the afternoon and we walked in the town till 6 o'clock, dinner time, after which we went to the Theatre Royal to see *Jo*, Jennie Lee is a wonderful little actress with a keen appreciation of the 'pathetic' and ludicrous part of life. I was not the only one of a great number who was privately weeping in the half light.

July 18th
This morning we went on an expedition we have long promised ourselves, viz. to buy two Swiss watches for our darling boys, and Captain Kidler has kindly offered to take the package as far as London. I can fancy their delight on receiving them! I wish I could see their beaming faces.

After luncheon we met Mrs Ridley and had a most lovely walk as far as 'Mrs Macquarie's Chair', which is a seat cut out of solid rock at the end of a road planned by one of the Governor's wives and named after her – 1845. The road skirts the Botanical Gardens, which are specially lovely as the harbour comes up to them and is only divided by a substantial stone wall low enough for everyone to enjoy the beauty of the water and the pretty little boats skimming about with the large ships and the steamers in the distance.[17]

July 20th
Went on board the *Cuzco* to say goodbye to Captain Kidler. Mr Carter and Mr Ridley went with us. The Captain was not on board, we found, but the purser entertained us right royally and showed us everything of interest: the frozen meat, the store room, chart room, steering gear worked by electricity, the lovely illuminated testimonial presented by the passengers to the captain. We left the ship at 4 o'clock as there was a great bustle and confusion with the passengers and their luggage coming on board as the *Cuzco* was about to start her homeward voyage. We were engaged to go to a dance with the Lockwoods this evening but Harry was unfortunately obliged to go to Newcastle for a day on business, so I went and enjoyed it immensely, returning to Mrs Lockwood's to sleep.

July 21st
Mrs Lockwood and I came over on the ferry in time for lunch at Tenby House, then we started on the steam tram for Botany Bay. Hearing a band of music, we turned into the

Sir Joseph Banks Gardens, they are prettily laid out, leading down to the beach. There is a large pavilion where dancing and drinking were going on – the company was not aristocratic but well-behaved and appeared to be thoroughly enjoying the half holiday.

There was a great display of pretty feet and shoes, and very good dancing. Having looked for about an hour, we went on to the beach. It is a rather dreary-looking bay, flat country and very white sand. Like Sydney and Melbourne, the entrance to it is very narrow, and there is a quantity of brown seaweed which looks like dried grass or straw.

At 5 o'clock we took up our station to wait for the train, which arrived <u>crowded</u> so we had to stand on the platform between the engine and the carriage. The clouds of steam that enveloped us most of the way were very unpleasant, I don't know which was the worst: that, or the cutting wind that we met at every corner of the streets!

July 22nd
Harry came back from Newcastle this morning. We went to dine with the Lockwoods, but having promised to meet Miss Bullions by the *Buniyong*, we left the North Shore soon after tea, coming across the bay by one of the steamers. It was raining heavily, so not a very pleasant journey. We then took a Hansom to the wharf, arriving just in time to see the lights of the steamer coming in. Mr Vale was with her also, and he and Miss B returned to Tenby House with us.

July 23rd
Went shopping in the morning. After lunch we took the tram to Coogee Bay, scrambled about the rocks and gathered some white heath. Then we sat down and ate some delicious mandarin oranges until it was time to head back to Sydney. The afternoon was cold and very windy but the sky perfectly clear, and the breakers came rolling in magnificently.

July 24th

An exquisite morning. Harry, Mr Vale, Miss Bullions and I walked to the Botanical Gardens, which are truly lovely, and sat under a tree with the Harbour spreading out like a picture before us. Every description of ship, from the stately Man of War lying at anchor, to the smallest sailing boats skimming along like a toy. It was quite an effort to retrace our steps to town along the Circular Quay, where we passed the splendid French steamer *Caledonian* and the P & O *Pekin*.

After lunch we took a steamer to Watson's Bay and walked up to the 'Gap' where the *Dunbar* was wrecked in '61. The rocks are very bold and although a perfectly calm day, the breakers boiled and roared incessantly. I cannot imagine what it must be in stormy weather! Then we walked to the Lighthouse on the South Head. It was a steep pull, uphill all the way, but we were rewarded by the lovely views. We hoped to see over the Lighthouse and its arrangements for electric lighting, but we were too late, so retraced our steps to the landing stage where the steamer was lying for the return journey. As is usual here, the weather was exquisite and the air perfectly clear.

After dinner we went to the theatre to see Jennie Lee[18] in *Grasshopper*. She is a clever little woman: last week we were shedding tears over *Jo*, and *Grasshopper* kept us in a perpetual state of merriment.

July 25th

Took the boat to Lavender Bay. When we arrived there we had to climb a <u>very</u> steep hill with steps cut in the rock. A seat was placed halfway, of which we all availed ourselves. We walked round to Milson's Point and on the rocks found a number of small oysters. The few we succeeded in knocking off were delicious. We called on Mrs Lockwood who gave us a cup of tea, which was very acceptable after the long walk.

We dined at 6, then went to see the Court Minstrels, which I must confess was <u>great rubbish</u> as an entertainment.

July 26th
We went by steamer up the Parramatta River to Parramatta. It was a cold journey but the coast is extremely pretty. Directly after we landed we passed some magnificent camellias. We lunched at the Woolpack Hotel where there was a rather large party, and we saw a Miss Gisborne who came out to Melbourne with us last year.

Being told we could walk to an orangery not far off, we started but found it some distance, and a very dusty road, so did not enjoy that part of the day.

The omnibus took us from Parramatta to the landing stage, where we found our steamer awaiting us, and we made the return journey through the delicious twylight. The wind had quite dropped, the outline of the trees, the twinkling lights of an occasional house, and the splashing of the paddle wheels in the smooth water, all tended to a most enjoyable passage down the river.

Harry was obliged to return to Newcastle tonight so went on board the *Morpeth* about 10.30. We all went to see him off. I am remaining until next week when Miss Bullions will return with me to Newcastle.

July 27th
I sat in the Botanical Gardens all morning. A dreadfully dusty, windy day, it causes the greatest amount of discomfort, and I don't wonder at people taking refuge in gauze veils and spectacles, as I saw several.

In the afternoon I went by bus to 'Hordern's Palace Emporium'. It is a very fine shop and one can spend an hour or so very well there, and the attendants are not at all pressing that you should buy things. Went to see *Proof* at the Gaiety. It is a pretty play and some of the acting very good, but I did not care for the stars, Sandiman and Miss Beaudet.

July 28th
I walked around town and saw over the Town Hall. In the afternoon to Botany Bay again – too windy for the beach, so sat in the garden which was very pleasant with quantities of violets and other flowers. Mr Vale left by the night boat for Newcastle.

July 29th Sunday
Miss Bullions and I went to the Roman Catholic Cathedral. It is a fine building and some of the singing was very good but the half-soiled red cassocks of the boys and their lace trimmings looked very tawdry. And when in an English cathedral in the afternoon, the singing was not so showy, the whole service seemed so much more <u>real</u>, though less of a spectacle. There were three dear little babies christened. We attended St Phillip's in the evening. A dull service and indifferent singing by the choir.

July 29th
Miss Bullions and I being left to our own devices, spent the morning in <u>business</u>, first packing, paying our hotel bill at Tenby House, then went to the steamer office and took our places and paid fares for the *Morpeth*, which was to sail at 11 pm. We came back to Tenby House for lunch at 1 o'clock, then into town for one or two errands, and treated ourselves to some custard apples, which are most delicious.

About 3.30 we went down to Circular Quay for the steamer to take us to Milson's Point, having promised to take tea with Mrs Lockwood. It was a most enjoyable little trip across the harbour. At 10 o'clock Mr and Mrs L brought us back to Sydney and we went on board the *Morpeth*.[19] Unfortunately the rain came on, but they would wait until we left the pier side. We stayed on deck until through the heads, being anxious to see the electric light in the Lighthouse. Just then a most uncomfortable swell and tumbled sea met the steamer and I found it necessary to beat a rapid retreat.

In the ladies saloon every bunk was filled by a prostrate form, and the most extraordinary medley of hats, cloaks, bags, umbrellas parcels etc. etc. lay on the table, and the grey-haired prim stewardess was wandering about and addressing everyone 'My dear'. I climbed into bed and lay down resigned to the sound of the machinery, groaning neighbours, and the occasional cries of a little girl who evidently felt very uncomfortable, and the mother had to attend to a tiny baby.

About 5 o'clock everyone seemed to awake with one accord, as we were nearly at our journey's end. Miss Bullions and I did not dress so early as Harry had promised to come on board at 8 am.

July 30th

We breakfasted on board the *Morpeth*. Harry came in good time and we started on our way up the Hunter River as far as the town of Morpeth. The country on either side is very pretty, especially the patches cultivated for the growth of lucerne grass, which is of the most brilliant green colour. The Indian corn is pretty also, and there were great numbers of pumpkins lying on the ground near the cottages.

The river winds about in the most wonderful way, as the steward expressed it, 'It is a regular snake of a river'. At one part we saw some dingoes, the first I had seen in a wild state. They were moving in a restless way with their tails in the air, and except for the shape of their tails might have been a party of foxes. A little further on, we saw a cow and calf that had drowned on the edge of the river when flooded. The dingoes were probably after them and tracking their way.

In going about the country in Australia, one misses the birds so much. An occasional magpie or laughing jackass was all we saw.

Ticket for the voyage on board the Morpeth.

Arrived at Morpeth about 12. Dined on board the steamer, then walked to the railway station, which was the smallest and most primitive I have ever seen. We took our places for Maitland, which is the next place, and a prettily laid-out town. Having twenty minutes to spare before starting for Newcastle, we got into a sort of omnibus, a wagonette that was waiting and drove around the town. The streets were broad and well laid out. There is an avenue of Morton Bay fig trees up to the Court House, and the gaol is built beside it. As we passed there were about half a dozen prisoners at work on the road, a warder with a fixed bayonet keeping guard. It seemed a pity those men could not have been working <u>honestly</u> for <u>themselves</u>, instead of being marked as prisoners with an armed man over them. Most of them had very low faces, but one or two had a good expression. The sun was shining brightly and they seemed to be taking their work very easily. Altogether their lot did not seem a hard one!

We reached the station just in time for our train. The nine hours spent in the steamer, in addition to the fresh air, excitement and actual fatigue began to tell on us, and both Miss Bullions and I kept dropping asleep in the train, and were really glad to arrive at Newcastle about 4 o'clock and I found myself once more on the *Superb* after an absence of more than a fortnight. I lay down on the bed till teatime at 5.30, after which we had a rubber of whist, but feeling very sleepy went to bed about 9.

August 1st
I spent the morning unpacking. After dinner Mr Vale took Miss Bullions and I on shore in the boat. It was pleasant rowing down to the landing stage. After some little difficulty we found the tennis ground. A few gentlemen were playing but the grass was very wet. After tea, whist and euchre.

August 2nd
I stayed on board all morning, I sat on the deck and worked. In the afternoon Harry went ashore with us, and we walked out as far as 'Nobby's' and to the end of the breakwater to see the immense blocks of stone brought down on a truck, one at a time and precipitated into the sea. Some of them were from fifteen to twenty hundred weight. It will take about five years to complete the breakwater.

August 3rd
I worked all morning. In the afternoon Harry went with us in the boat over to Stockton, which is immediately opposite to where the *Superb* is now lying. A few wretched houses occupied by lime-burners chiefly, and coal stokers, form the town, but seeing some beautiful beach beyond, decided to walk across through some scrub and bracken fern. Sand was everywhere, and how anything could <u>grow</u> there I cannot think. We were going slowly along, the sun being very hot, and just glancing about for anything in the shape of a flower or pretty form when we were most unpleasantly surprised

by the sight of a large black snake just in front of us. It must have been six feet long, it was partly coiled up with head erect and tongue out. We did not care to see any more, so retraced our steps and kept to the beaten track, which led us to the beach. There were some rather pretty shells, which we filled our pockets with. The sandy beach appears to extend for some miles and looks beautifully white with the blue sea at one edge and dark scrub in the background. On coming back to the jetty, we found the boat awaiting us, two of the midshipmen who went off with guns had not returned so we left them behind. Later in the evening the boat went back to fetch them but they came empty-handed as regards game!

August 4th
Miss Bullions and I worked all morning, walked the deck etc. We intended going on shore after dinner, but heavy rain came on. After tea we played Euchre and Whist in the saloon, danced between decks.

August 5th Sunday
Harry, Mr Vale, Miss Bullions and I went to Christ Church Cathedral from which there is a beautiful view. The service was primitive, but thoroughly congregational and an excellent sermon from the Reverend Selwyn on the tendency of the present time to place Science and Reason in place of Faith and Religion!

August 6th
Mr Vale, Miss B and I went for a walk on the breakwater. Harry came to meet us. I sat on deck all afternoon, lovely weather. Played Whist in the evening.

August 7th
The ship hauled alongside the wharf and coal commenced coming in. It was very dusty and unpleasant. Mr Lopez gave us a Dingo. It is a beautiful creature but very wild at present, just like a wolf, but we hope to be able to tame it.

August 8th
We stayed on board all morning, after dinner we went for
a very pleasant drive in Mr Thomson's buggy. We called
at his house (the butcher's shop) for the buggy, he invited
us upstairs to see his wife and baby! But our noses were
assailed by all sorts of horrid odours, and we were not long
to find ourselves on the balcony, where we were introduced to the Baby, also a very small monkey. Finally we
started for the drive, Mr Barker riding on a grey pony. Mr
T took us to the 'Folly', where we strolled about among
the orange trees, drank new milk, and he gave us lovely
bunches of flowers and a <u>branch</u> of oranges. Then he took
us to another garden where the proprietor was hard at
work among his men. One tree of mandarin oranges was
an extraordinary sight, being a <u>mass of fruit</u>. About one
fourth of it had been cleared and yielded <u>150 dozen,</u> but
they were of a kind more suited for preserving than eating
raw. He then gave us a lovely bouquet each and as many
red and white camellias as we could carry. It was a great
joke getting into the buggy again as our hands were full of
flowers and our pockets so full of fruit we could hardly
sit down.

We arrived on board in time for tea, after which we again
went to town to the theatre, having taken tickets for the
Benefit of Miss Rosa Towers. It was a poor affair, and the
only interesting part was given by a Professor Rice who calls
himself a 'thought reader', and certainly led people to the
objects they were thinking of.

August 9th
We were shewn the fortifications. There are seven guns,
three 12 ton guns and four 80 pounders. The subterranean
passages were about 30 feet underground and solid stone
with ventilation at intervals.[20]
In the afternoon we went to the cathedral to hear the
Bishop of Newcastle but as the address was to young girls

there was not much scope for his eloquence – if he has any. Played Whist in the evening.

August 10th
Mail for England leaves today. I posted a letter to Harold and newspapers to Jesse. The Darlings, how my heart yearns for their love and caresses.

We went into town and bought a large sunshade hat for the voyage, and a few other little things. Harry has bought a goat for me to have the milk. When she arrived on board there was great excitement among the dogs. The puppy was very impudent and kept barking around. At length nanny caught him with her horns and sent him off yelping!

August 11th
The coal is now all on, and the hatches fastened down. We were towed from the Dyke this morning into the stream where we shall remain at anchor till Monday. This afternoon we went to a football match between Sydney and Newcastle, the latter were victorious, so are now champions of New South Wales.

August 12th Sunday
We are still lying at anchor in the stream, and as this is Sunday we cannot get away today. Harry had to meet some gentlemen in town with regard to an intending passenger who has not made his appearance, so Miss B, Mr Vale and I went to St John's Church for morning service, extending our walk thither round by the cliffs, which give a view that is always fresh, the great breakers of the South Pacific rolling up to the rocks so grandly! The sun was shining brightly, and we had a good half hour's walk to church. St John's is evidently more <u>fashionable</u> than the Cathedral, but somehow I prefer the primitiveness of the latter with

the hearty singing of the <u>children</u>, to the more finished choir and modern style of St John's.

We found the boat at the wharf waiting for us, rather a rough sea but we got on board without a wetting just in time for dinner.

During the morning another splendid Dingo had been brought on board, of a dull yellow colour, with ears erect and waving bushy tail. There was some difficulty getting him up the ladder as he did not understand the proceeding and resented it. As he stood at bay with his wolf-like mouth open displaying a very good set of teeth, matters were brought to a standstill. However, someone thought of the boathooks[21] and the butcher, steward etc. managed to bring him on board at last. Once there he was perfectly good-humoured and allowed us all to stroke and pat him, but everyone evinced some caution in going near at first. Dingoes are great enemies of sheep and fowls so will have to be kept on a chain. I have named one 'Onabegamba' (the native name of a small island opposite Newcastle of which 'Oomebah' is the native name). The Australian names I have heard are all soft and musical, such as Woolhara, Wooloomooloo, Waratah, Coogee, Wonga Wonga, You Yangs, Mitti Mitti, Bulli, Wollongong, but the few aborigines I have seen are very ugly and uninteresting[22] with the exception of one young fellow on the wharf at Newcastle who looked intelligent and was well-dressed.

I must not omit to mention the action of one old black fellow, which was worthy of a Prince! He had a bunch of crimson camellias in his hand, and I casually admired them in passing with a friend. He immediately separated some and offered them with a bow. Of course we accepted them with thanks, and while I was wondering whether to offer him some money, he had passed on in the crowd, and I believe had given them to us in pure good nature!

But I have wandered from Dingoes to Blacks! and I must come back to our last Sunday evening in port. Miss B played some lovely sonatas on the piano, but we both felt rather sad at the prospect of parting tomorrow. We have no doctor on board, so she cannot make the return voyage with us owing to her delicate throat.

August 13th
Everything is in preparation for starting, the anchor having been weighed, signals hoisted for tug and pilot. The last visitor to the ship will be the shipping clerk with final business papers. Miss B will return to shore with him and start tonight for Sydney in the *Morpeth*. She and I are both rather inclined to weep at the thought of saying goodbye so soon.

August 14th
The tug took us yesterday about 1.30 so Mr Molton and Miss B went off in the little sailing boat to the shore. We waved our handkerchiefs until we lost sight of her. Then I ran to the cabin for the glasses thinking I might distinguish her on the wharf. All this time we have been rapidly approaching 'Nobby's' and the breakwater, when to my delight there stood Mr M and Miss B on the extremity of the breakwater in time to see us pass through. More waving of hats and handkerchiefs, but the distance between us was steadily increasing, and very soon I could only see the dim outline of the shore even with the glasses. The sails were set, the pilot and tug left and we were once more 'at sea'. A splendid fair wind took us away from the land before night fell. I stayed on deck till bedtime, walking about and <u>trying</u> to regain my sea legs! Everyone seemed in rather a staggery condition! And I suppose it will be a few days before we are used to this 'curious up and down motion'.

August 15th

We passed a most miserable night, what with rolling oneself, articles rolling in the other cabins, and all sorts of noises to which we have not yet become accustomed. Sleep was quite out of the question. I got up and dressed about 10 and felt very shaky and squeamish. I managed to sit on deck till dinnertime when I had to retire to bed. Poor old Boxer and the white cat kept me company, both I fancy feeling rather <u>invalidish</u>!

August 18th

I was feeling decidedly better today and able to appreciate the weather, which had been unbroken since leaving Newcastle, but the wind being <u>aft</u> has caused some rolling, however we are speeding on our way, which is a comfort!

A few Cape pigeons are following us, and last night a fine flying fish came on board, 14 inches long. The carpenter took his wings and the steward had the fish cooked for his breakfast this morning, it is very delicate and delicious.

Boxer had a fight with one of the dingoes today. I was afraid he would be killed, the dingoes being twice his size. Both were badly bitten but the butcher managed to separate them before anything was done. There is quite a menagerie on board: seven dogs, five goats, two cats, two kittens, and dozens of Australian cockatoos and parrots, as well as the sheep, pigs, fowls and ducks for consumption on the voyage.

August 19th Sunday

We had Divine Service in the saloon at 10.30. A small congregation compared to the one on the outward voyage. We sang 'Eternal Father'. Afterwards I sat on deck till dinnertime, lovely sunshine, blue sky and sea, with the waves breaking as white as snow against the ship's side.

It seems very strange being the only lady on board, but everyone is very nice and agreeable and I must do plenty of work. Until yesterday I have been too <u>queer</u> to take any interest in anything. Mackenzie came in to dinner today, and we are going to ask all the midshipmen in the saloon one evening this week for some music and cards for those who are not musical.

Continued fine weather and fair wind. In the evening a little land bird was blown on board. Several tried to catch it, but though much exhausted it managed to keep out of reach, and would no doubt be drowned as the wind is too strong for it to return to New Zealand where it probably came from.

Dist 142

August 21st <u>Antipodes Day</u>
Still fine and pleasant. I sat on deck all morning and most of the afternoon. In the evening Mr Mackenzie and Mr Hills and all the midshipmen came to tea and we spent the evening in music. I played accompaniments *ad lib.* and one rubber was formed.

Lat 34° 19' S Long 177° 10' W Dist 172

August 23rd
A gale blowing from the SW. The ship is jumping about, seas coming over, and everything miserable. I did not get up till midday and then felt so queer I had to lie down again. The outer jib was split and one of the upper topsails. The main top mast stay and post forward shroud were carried away. We were shipping heavy seas and sprays.

August 24th
The wind has moderated, but high seas and the ship rolling heavily. Sleep is almost out of the question. Seas were washing about the deck and occasional heavy sprays on the poop. Finished a Tam O'Shanter cap for Harry.

Lat 35° 28' Long 167° 8' Dist 201.

August 25th
Weather much finer, I sat on deck all morning, and narrowly escaped a wetting several times.
   Dist 124 miles

August 26th 1883
The fourteenth anniversary of our wedding day! It seems wonderful to look back upon so many years, so much has happened, and yet in a sense so short. How many have passed away from our circle since that memorable day to us in 1869, and two have entered it, our darling boys!
   Service in the saloon 10.30, only one hymn.
   Lat 34° 19' Long 158° 6' Dist 237

August 28th
Very fine, and almost calm. Sat on deck all day. I saw a small whale.

August 29th
Still very fine with little wind. Mr Mackenzie, Mr Hollis and all the midshipmen came in to tea and we had music till 8.30 and one rubber of whist. Several 'mollys'[23] and pigeons around the ship.

August 30th
A strong wind sprang up on the morning watch. The ship was rolling and lurching all day. Harry thinks this is the South East Trade Wind that has set in, so has decided to make his course <u>through</u> the Society Islands instead of eastward of them as he originally intended.
   Lat 23° 12' Long 149° 50' Dist 204

September 1st
The sea has gone down, and the weather is lovely. We entered the Tropics today and already rejoice in the delicious balmy air, though not too warm. Tonight we passed

between two of the Islands, Toubouai and Vivatou. They were about thirty miles distant and being night time, Harry kept us as far from each as possible. Hoping to get a good view of Tahiti if we can only pass by daylight.

Lat 24° 33' Long 148° 58' Dist 229

September 2nd Sunday
We had the service in the saloon, morning and evening. Several of the sailors attended and we had hearty singing, 'Rock of Ages', 'Jesu Lover of my soul' and 'Sun of my soul' in the evening. After service I sat on deck by starlight until 10 pm. A fair fresh breeze, soft and balmy.

The new moon as Harry quoted:

'... But, motionless, As 'twere an angel's shallop[24] in a calm,
The bent moon floats and its round freight of hope
Lies in its breast – to unbelieving eyes
A shadow that can never grow more fair,
–But, to the clearer sighted stars, a promise
Of brightness that will wax to fill a heaven.'[25]

One sees the full beauty of the moon and stars in these tropical evenings, and thank a poet for expressing what we feel when we cannot put admiration in words for ourselves, or even thoughts.

Lat 21° 48' Long 148° 58' Dist 165

September 3rd
Much warmer, we are speeding along with the South East Trades. We had the deadlight open, and found the awning spread on deck. I spent all morning trimming a 'shady' hat. Land was reported about 5 pm and one and all are disappointed that we shall pass Tahiti in the night, as it is the principal island of the group. Only the dim outline was visible, and the sun setting about 5.30, it was very soon dark. I sat on deck til 9 pm when a sharp squall of wind and rain

came up. It is very warm in the saloon and cabins when the deadlights are closed again.

Lat 19° 12' Long 148° 52' Dist 156

September 4th
We passed Tahiti about midnight, and the fates seem against one seeing anything of these islands as we are now about 80 miles from the next one, and we shall pass that in the night too! However it is a great mercy we have come through them so well, for looking at the chart they seem to be so thickly grouped together.

Lat 16° 5' Long 148° 45' Dist 187

September 6th
The weather is hotter each day, but a strong breeze. The air here seems more moist and cloudy than in the Atlantic, and when the moon rises there is generally a mist over her for a time. It is impossible to express the lassitude I experience in these latitudes. With all the beautiful scenery of a tropical country I should not like to live in one.

While seated at dinner, today we heard a <u>dreadful</u> thump on deck over head. For a second we all looked at each other, then Harry, Mr Barker and Mr Vale rushed on deck, and found their fears realised. Poor Villard (known as Frenchy) had fallen from the mizen rigging about 30 feet. He was taken up senseless, with bad cuts in his head, face and arm, but after examination, they hoped he had no bones broken. After a time he recovered consciousness and he was laid on a bed on the poop, being cooler than the Forecastle. It was so sad to see him lying there, though everyone is surprised he was not killed or very <u>severely</u> injured.

Lat 10° 7' Long 148° 40' Dist 180

September 7th
We are now clear of all land and speeding our way north towards the line. I played quoits with Mr Dove and worked

all day at my '5 o'clock tea cloth'. I sat on deck all evening, it was rather cloudy but too hot to go below till bed time. Lat 7° 47' Dist 150

September 8th
Not quite as hot after a shower of rain. Played quoits morning and evening. Heavy rain came on about 7 o'clock, but in Harry's oilskin over my own waterproof I sat through it, perfect rivers running off the edge of my hat, and I had to stuff my handkerchief inside the collar of my coat to keep the water from trickling down <u>inside</u> my dress, but anything is preferable to the <u>heat below</u>!

9th September Sunday
A lovely morning, air cooler and brighter. I was awoken last night by one of the dogs yelping and screaming as though terribly hurt, and heard this morning that poor little Judy died in a <u>fit</u>. She was born on the outward voyage and a most affectionate and comical little mongrel. Poor Judy.

10th September
We crossed the line this evening. A nice fair breeze. Quoits, work, and read Mark Twain's *A Tramp Abroad*. Villard progressing very well. Lat 25' Long 148° 56' Dist 158

September 11th
We crossed the line last night and now we are in a <u>North</u> latitude! It is really overwhelming to think we shall have to come <u>twice</u> through the tropics before reaching dear England again! Played quoits on the main deck with Mr Dove, Mackenzie and Hills. Sat on deck till 9 pm.

September 12th
The sun is <u>vertical</u> today, very hot, being 80° in the shade at 11 am. I thoroughly appreciate the Chinese lounger in this weather that Harry bought in Newcastle. Dist 138 miles

September 13th
Hotter than ever! Went on deck about 8.30 am. Two Bo'sun birds have been with us for a day or so. Pretty birds with one solitary feather sticking out of their tails. I wonder what it is for! About 12 o'clock, hearing a cry of 'Shark Ho!' I ran up on the poop, being just in the act of looking at our position on the chart. There was Mr Shark paddling quietly alongside, or astern. The hook and line were soon thrown over which he eagerly seized. They managed to get him half way up the ship's side when the hook straightened and he splashed into the water, no doubt to his own satisfaction!

A fresh hook was put over, but after nibbling the bait, he kept a discreet distance and soon left us.

Heavy squalls of rain all day at intervals.

Lat 4° N, Long 148° 29'

September 16th Sunday
Oh the miseries of the <u>'Doldrums'</u>! Drenching, pouring rain, stifling heat in the cabin, the ship rolling on the swell and to crown all the dead lights closed!

So the choice lies between being wet to the skin or almost suffocated below. I generally prefer the former.

A dolphin or Coryphene[26] was caught on Friday, seen in the water alongside. It was the most <u>exquisite and brilliant blue.</u> The Bo'sun caught it on the Fo'csle and everyone ran to see it. Then I realised the beauty of the changing hues of the 'dying dolphin' – golden spots on a blue ground, blue spots on a gold colour, a lovely pink shade and patches of black rapidly succeeded each other. He was soon cut up, which I did not stay to see, but I was greedy or curious enough to taste him at tea time, all his glory dispatched, served on a dish surrounded by <u>melted butter</u> instead of darting about in almost limitless space in the Pacific Ocean. He tasted rather tough and dry.

Lat 10° 45' Long 145° 21' Dist 71 miles

Maud's sketch of the Coryphene.

September 17th
To the delight of everyone we got the North East Trades last night. The fresh air seemed to lift a weight off one, both physically and mentally! Still very hot, but the breeze makes it bearable.
    Lat 12° 12' Long 146° 7' Dist 96

September 18th
Cooler and lovely weather. Quoits on deck in the morning.
    Lat 15° 16' Long 147° 16' Dist 191

September 19th
Moderate breeze, still rather hot. A few flying fish seen.
    Lat 17° 42' Long 148° 57' Dist 179

September 20th
Moderate breeze, getting gradually cooler. Lovely moonlight and starlight nights just now.
    Lat 20 16' Long 150 18' Dist 172

Sept 27th
Lat 31° 34' Long 141° 23' Dist 148

October 1st
Strong fair breeze and signs of approaching land. I was awoken this morning by that old familiar sound of the cable being hauled up. It is so delightful to think of being so soon in port, and <u>then our letters!</u> We are flying along at a rate of 10 or 11 knots an hour.

October 2nd
Still the strong wind and we expect to sight the 'Farallones'[26] lighthouse this afternoon. It is so exciting rushing through the water, when every hour brings us nearer our destination. 2 pm, two sails in sight, and land reported from aloft, it is the lighthouse! 2.30 the light-house is distinctly visible, getting nearer every moment. A range of forbidding-looking rocks with the lighthouse perched on the highest, 350 feet high.

The Pilot cutter sighted about 3.30. The Pilot was watched with the greatest anxiety and curiosity. A square-built, fresh-coloured man with wide-awake hat, <u>goatee</u> beard and square-toed boots, he has not a superfluous word for anyone, while we were brimful of excitement and would like to ask a hundred questions!

Our voyage to 'Frisco is virtually at an end, we are entering the 'Golden Gate' after nightfall, a great disappointment, but I must begin a new book with our introduction to California!

M B 2nd October 1883.

<u>Notes</u> [on the back of the diary]
  Jessie P Bullions
  Wilson's Institution for Hospital Trained Nurses
  96 Wimpole Street
  Cavendish Square London
  Maud Berridge (Timperley)

Two months in San Francisco and the return voyage to England

Commencing October 3rd 1883
I concluded the last volume of my diary under the impression that we were entering the 'Golden Gate' in the darkness, however in a few minutes I heard the rattle of the anchor being let go, and when I went on deck, Harry told me that the Pilot had decided to anchor for the night. I felt so pleased, as we should, I knew, not make another start before daylight, and I determined to be up, however early. We walked about the deck, looking at the outline of the coast, trying to realise that we were looking at <u>America.</u> The night was exceptionally clear and fine, as fogs are extremely frequent on the coast and dreaded very much by the Captains of ships. The Pilot became quite talkative, having finished his work for the night, and answered all our questions. His replies were frequently commenced by 'Well, I guess...' so and so, in agreeing with a question, he said, 'That's so.' He had a peculiar slow manner of speaking, almost nasal but not quite, but what astonished me more than anything was the free and easy style he had of <u>spitting</u> right and left. At first I tried to look as though it was a matter of course, but I very soon found it <u>was</u> a matter of course in 'Frisco.

We went to bed about 11, quite tired with the excitement of the day, or I was. The first night in berth is so strangely quiet without the usual rushing by of the water, or trampling overhead!

This morning about 6 am I was awoken by the weighing of the anchor. I got up at once and dressed, hurried on deck. There was a heavy mist, all the woodwork was very wet and deck also. In a little while the tug took us, and we were really through the Golden Gate. The sun shone through the mist, a pale yellow colour.

I met with a very good description of the entrance and harbour in *Harper's Magazine*, to copy it into my diary:

All at once occurs an opening through bold mountainous range on the very water's edge, and we are at the famed Golden Gate of San Francisco.

It is a mere eyelet of a strait, but it gives access to a wide expanse of bay. So happy is the opening and so commodious the shelter that the reversal of the churlish tradition by which the shore has been governed up to this point, seems quite startling.

There is no room for doubt, when once the site is known, as to why San Francisco is located where it is. It has the only natural harbour between Astoria, Oregon, seven hundred miles north of it, and San Diego six hundred miles to the southward. It has with this advantage such a relation to the resources of the country behind it, that it could not escape a destiny of greatness if it would. It is not simply a bay upon which we enter, but an inland sea with a commerce of its own. There are islands in point – round-backed Goat and Angel Islands like sea monsters gone to sleep, and terraced Alcatraz, with its citadel as picturesque as a bit of Malta.

Far vistas open beyond them on many sides, and there are white cities and low lying areas of smoky atmosphere.

San Francisco, itself close at hand, bristles up sharply from numerous hills. The waterfront is wild with shipping: craft of all shapes and sizes cut across one another's tracks in the harbour. The Lateen sails of Maltese and Genoese fishermen and the junks of Chinese shrimp catchers figure among them.

Ferry boats of a pattern much superior as a rule to any thing we are familiar with in the East ply to the suburb of Oakland, already a city of fifteen thousand people and sometimes called the City of Churches, to Alameda with its esplanade of white bathing pavilions; to Berkeley with its handsome university buildings and institution for the deaf and dumb, and to rustic Saracito and San Rafael under the shade of dark Mount Tamalpais.

Yonder from Oakland projects the interminable pier of the Central Pacific Railway, it is a mile in length. As we come up we see in turn the Palace Hotel, the Market Street Shot Tower, and the houses of the great millionaires who have made such a stir in their day and generation. Three or four of these crown California Street, or 'Nob Hill'[1] as it is called. They are chiefly those of the railway and mining kings. 'Nob Hill' is three hundred feet high, Telegraph Hill nearly as high, and Russian Hill behind the first, also coming into favour as a residence is three hundred and sixty. How in the world do millionaires and others get up to their imposing homes? All in good time, we shall see. .... It is indeed an inland sea, this bay. You can go southward upon it thirty miles, northward as far, and thirty miles northeastward also to the Straits of Carqùinez! With Benicia on one side, and Martinez the point of departure for the ascent of the high peak of Mount Diablo, on the other – and through these straits into Suisun Bay, which receives the waters of the Sacramento and San Joaquin rivers, and is in itself twenty miles long in addition.

How strange it is arriving from the other side of the world, to find the mill of people waiting at the edge of the dock all dressed in the usual way, and chattering in the familiar speech even to bits of the current slang! A China steamer, however, has come in just before us and supplies a sufficient element of foreigners. The almond-eyed Celestials in their loose wide-sleeved coats are swarming down her sides and about her decks. Groups of them are loaded into express wagons and driven up town with the convoy of friends who have come to meet them. Others trudge slowly away on foot, with their effects deposited in a pair of wicker baskets, one at each end of a long bamboo rod supported on their shoulders. This is [a] way of carrying a burden constantly met with in the town especially among the vegetable dealers, who hawk their wares from house to house. The figures thus equipped present exactly the aspect of those shewn us on the cuts of the labourers in the tea fields. It is poor travelling when curiosity alone and not the imagination is gratified, and San Francisco promises ample material for both.

I must now return to my own experience. Breakfast over at about 10 o'clock. Harry was ready to go on shore on the *Thetis*, a steam yacht waiting alongside, and I gladly availed myself of the opportunity of going too, with the hope of getting our <u>letters</u>. With a small scramble down the ship's side, we were soon on our way to the wharf and landed at a place almost monopolised by Italian fishermen with their Lateens.[2]

Captain Bingham, one of the stevedores, was awaiting us with a Buggy in which there was only room for two, so he took me to the office, Harry following in another Buggy.

The pavement of the streets is dreadful, consisting of large <u>round</u> stones, so we bumped along in a manner quite new to me, but the springs of the Buggy were very strong, also the wood they are made of, as indeed it need be. Arrived at the office I was marched through a crowd of ship's captains into an inner room where I was introduced to Mr Menzies the other partner, a Scotchman, <u>Americanized</u>. He was very polite and soon had our bundles of home letters ready for me, then kindly left me to the perusal of them. Harry was being taken about and introduced all round, and congratulated on the splendid passage we had made from Newcastle: fifty days. Having had 'good news from home' and posted some letters I had ready, I felt on the *qui vive* to see all the new sights of 'Frisco, but Mr Menzies kindly insisted on lunching at his house, so we got into another buggy, and we were rattled over the stones, were swerved over the car lines in rather a startling manner, up a <u>very</u> steep hill, and was welcomed by Mrs Menzies at the door. All the houses are built of wood, but at first sight are a good deal like the low-windowed houses of London, except for the steepness of the hills.

From the drawing room we looked into the street, which would have been commonplace but for the fact that the opposite house was reached by an approach of about <u>fifty</u> steps as near as I could count. When we went into the dining room I exclaimed at the beauty of the view, for this house, like so many others was on the side of a hill with the front looking at the street and the back seemed to be hanging over the harbour. Mountains in front of us, islands and shipping far below.

We had a pleasant luncheon: grilled chicken, quail on toast, delicious bread, butter, cake, preserved and fresh fruits and tea of a peculiar flavour, but after a time we got to like it. Mrs Menzies was very friendly, not in the least bit formal as an English stranger is apt to be, thoroughly American in voice and manners: 'I guess'; 'Is that so?' sounding very strange to us. In the middle of the afternoon we returned to the ship and spent the evening on board.

October 4th
Went on shore with Harry in the morning and went to Mr Daly's office. He took us into town, the streets are busy and the shops very fine. At 12 o'clock we went to the Royal Restaurant for lunch. The longer part of the dining hall was for gentlemen and about a third for ladies and gentlemen, the latter part being waited on by n_____, on account, I was told, of their politeness. We took our places at one of the little tables and thoroughly enjoyed our lunch. There

was a plentiful bill of fare. The place was crowded, everyone laughing and talking and eating. Seeing one lady gnawing something from her fingers, I made enquiries of Mr Daly who told me it was 'green corn', and ordered some for me to taste, and told me to eat it in the orthodox manner, in my fingers, and it was really delicious. Unlike an English restaurant there was an abundance of fruit, vegetables, pickles, bread, butter, iced water included in the very moderate charge. This was a people's dining place and there was certainly a good deal of noise going on. And the cooking and attention were good, though the table linen was not of the finest, and though we afterwards lunched at grander places, I don't know that it was more enjoyable.

In the afternoon Mr Daly took us through Chinatown. Oh! The smells that greeted our noses, in some of the shops for eatables we saw horrid bits of fat strung on strings, also fish anything but fresh, vegetables that looked as though they had been gathered weeks ago. Such strange-looking sweetmeats in cases. Other shops had curios, some clothing, shoes etc. but the most amusing thing was to look into a barber's, generally in the basement where a Chinaman sat with the greatest gravity, while another shaved the front part of his head, and unplaited, brushed, combed and re-plaited his pigtail! We met a few women and children, they all wore a loose sort of jacket, very wide sleeves. It is only the fashion of the hair and something in the expression of the face that made me exclaim 'There's a Chinese woman'. They have their hair smooth as satin, done in large bows and generally ornamented pins stuck through. The children wear brighter colours and a sort of hood with two horns out of the top which give a most grotesque appearance! Though the horns are only bits of cloth. We went into a joss house. The entrance was up a dingy flight of wooden stairs, and we read a notice: 'Enter by this way to the Joss House of Hang Sen Tong', so we went up a few more stairs, and found a Chinaman in a small kind of office. We asked his permission to enter, which he gave at once with a serious sort of smile. We passed into a room hung round with very tawdry dangling signs, bronze bowls on a table, some fine carving, a frightful figure as a centrepiece, before which the joss stick was burning in a bowl, and some little lamps alight perpetually. The joss stick filled the room with a sickly smell, and I afterwards came to the conclusion that it was this mingled with opium smoke and eatables that produced the peculiar smell one always meets with on Chinese streets.

Oct 5th

Mr Daly kindly arranged for me to be driven through the Golden Gate Park, the buggy only holding two, Harry could not go today. The Park has been entirely <u>made</u> and considering that the site was a few years ago a succession of sand hills, is wonderfully fine. The roads are broad and splendidly laid out, large evergreens on either side, more in the middle of the park. There is a conservatory, lawn and flower beds prettily laid out. The grass was beautifully green owing to the great care taken of it, and is in strong contrast to the sandy hills and plains we passed on our way out of the park, the main road leading to the ocean beach <u>outside</u> the Golden Gate. We passed a good number of smart buggies and splendid horses, indeed I have been struck from the first with the beauty of the horses, such lovely coats and so well groomed. They are driven at a great speed along the smooth roads of the park, and it is quite a fashionable resort in the fine afternoon.

Oct 6th

Stayed on board all morning and wrote letters. After an early lunch Harry and I took the cars for Woodward's Gardens.[3] It is a sort of 'Zoo', a collection of animals, flower garden, and a large hall where there was a variety of entertainment going on, singing and dancing. We had heard a good deal of 'Woodwards' and were rather disappointed with it, but on the ornamental pond there was a curious circular boat which the children seemed to appreciate, as there was a pair of small oars at short intervals, and the little ones kept getting in and out and rowing for a few minutes with great energy.

Oct 7th

We have had perfect weather so far, and every morning when I go on deck there is a beautiful view spread out, of the harbour, islands, shipping, and at frequent intervals the large white ferries passing backwards and forwards, which are a sight in themselves. We arranged to go the Alameda, so took the ferry about 2 pm after taking our tickets at the booking office, we passed through a large waiting room and to our astonishment, on board the ferry, the gangway was the entire width of the stem of the boat, and on a level. Carriages and carts and horses drove quietly and took up their places for the passage. Most of the passengers made their way up a small staircase to the upper deck where there is also a splendid saloon upholstered in red plush with looking glasses at intervals and above all a plentiful supply of <u>spittoons</u>. Also a notice on the deck 'Gentlemen are requested <u>not</u> to spit on this deck as it is used by Ladies.' It is an extraordinary habit, even women seem afflicted with it.

We took our places on deck and thoroughly enjoyed the passage across to Oakland, again the ferry glided into its place, the crowd walked into the railway station, or as it is called, the Depot. There were immense trains waiting with different destinations hanging in front of the engine. Soon a large bell began to clang, and away we started. The bell continued to ring the whole way, as the cars run through the public road, stopping at certain intervals. Pretty houses are along the road, until we got into Alameda, which is a pretty little country town with a beautiful backdrop of mountains, the air so clear and the gardens full of autumn flowers. We sauntered about, everything seemed so quiet and tranquil, people had a sort of <u>Sunday</u> look about them, although most of the shops were open. We took the returning car about 4, which met the ferry, our journey across the bay being about 15 minutes. We arrived on board *Superb* in time for tea.

Oct 9th

I accepted an invitation to spend the day with Mrs Daly. Mr Daly took me to the house from town on the buggy. They live at Chattanooga, off 24th Street, such a funny address. Chattanooga is the name of one of the American victories, but I forget the general's name. I arrived at the house about 12. Such a pretty little cottage standing back from the street. In the garden quantities of heliotrope, fuchsias and roses. It was not a formal visit as Mrs Daly keeps no servant, so I went about the house with her, and we sat in the garden cutting 'string beans' with the lovely weather and convenient American stove it was really like playing at housekeeping. As we sat in the garden I saw for the first time in my life <u>Humming</u> birds flying from flower to flower. They look so lovely as they put their beaks into each of the fuchsia bells and balance themselves by their wings, the movement is so rapid that one could hardly distinguish it was a bird, until they dart off to the nest.

Harry and Mr Daly came in time for tea, after which we had some music. Miss Laffey, a young lady staying in the house, and Mrs Fitzgerald, a young widow living near came in for the evening. Mrs Daly kindly offered us a room so we stayed the night.

Oct 10th

It was delightful this morning on waking to throw open the window and let in the bright sunshine and smell the flowers! And such a change to run <u>downstairs</u> to breakfast, instead of walking out of our cabin into the saloon as we have done for so many weeks. Then the bread and butter and milk are so delicious. We were amused beyond everything at the size

of a slice of watermelon with which we <u>began</u> our breakfast. The rind is bright green, the flesh inside a rosy pink.
Some people eat great quantities and they are considered
very wholesome, but I should prefer them in hot weather.
The gentlemen went to town directly after breakfast. We
arranged a few household matters and followed a little later.
Then I had my first experience of a Cable Car. I extract a
description from *Harper's Monthly*:

> The San Francisco householder particularly has 'a
> station like the herald Mercury new lighted on some
> heaven-kissing hill'! How in the world, I have asked, does
> he get up there? Well then, by the cable roads. I should
> consider the cable road one of the very foremost on the
> list of curiosities, though I have been able to refrain from
> speaking from it. It is a peculiar kind of tramway, quite as
> useful on a level, but invented expressly for the purpose of
> overcoming steep elevations. Two cars, coupled together
> are seen moving at a high rate of speed, without jar and
> with perfect safety, up and down all the extraordinary
> undulations of the ground. They have no horse, no steam,
> no vestiges of machinery, no ostensible means of loco-
> motion. The astonished comments of the Chinaman,
> observing for the first time this marvel, old as it is, may be
> worth repeating once mere for its quaint force: 'Amelican
> man's wagon, no pushee, no pullee, all same go top side
> hill, like flashee.'
>   The solution of the mystery is in an endless wire cable
> hidden in a box in the road bed, and turning over a great
> wheel in an engine housed at the top of the hill. The fore-
> most of the cars is provided with a grip or pincers, running
> underneath it, through a continuous crevice in the same
> box as the cable, and managed by a conductor. When he
> wishes to go on, he clutches the always-moving cable and
> goes with it. If he wishes to stop, he simply lets go and
> puts on the brake.

Oct 11th
Spent the day with Mrs Brigham, after lunch she drove me
through the Golden Gate Park. It was a lovely day, and she
was anxious to return by a different route, asking the way
of a workman. He directed us but said he didn't know if we
could 'jump the track'. A new road was being made to the
beach, but we managed to drive over a few parts of it and
round the side of a mountain, I forget the name, but at one
angle we overlooked the town from a great height, which
was called 'Cape Horn', and as there was very little smoke
we could see right away to the harbour.

Oct 12th
We dined at Mr Menzies. There were several Captains there,
and we, or rather they, compared notes, of course, and had
a little music. Mrs Menzies sings extremely well, and has a
very rich voice.

Oct 13th
Today is the closing day of the Pacific Yachting Club, and
we were delighted to accept Mrs Menzies invitation to
Sausalito. We went in a steam yacht. The weather was rather
squally, and I think all the ladies were glad to land. Three
sailing yachts followed, each with a party on board. We
landed on a small landing stage, and ascended the hill. The
road was nicely laid out, ending in a garden in front of the
club house, which was an ornamental building, with a broad
verandah running around. We entered a splendid large room
which was on purpose for dancing, with waxed floor and
windows opening to the verandah. An elegant luncheon was
laid out in the dining room, about 150 sat down. I was rather
puzzled when a young lady asked me to pass the 'crackers'. I expected to find bonbons but could not see any, and
at once betrayed myself as <u>English</u>, as the dish of biscuits
was in front of me and are called crackers by all Americans.
Then we had clam chowder – which I was rather curious

to taste and found very good. Clams are a sort of oyster and made into a stew. After luncheon a delightful dance, but of course we did not know many people, so I had to endure the trial of listening to the music, sitting most of the time. Then prizes were given to the three winning gallettes – an ornamental wheel, a pennant and a silver flagon and of course some speechifying. We returned to San Francisco about 6 o'clock after a very pleasant day. We were delighted to get letters from home, one containing Jesse's likeness. It made me homesick to look at his saucy little face. Harold's was not quite finished, but to follow next week.

Oct 14th
In the morning Harry and I went with Mrs FitzGerald to church in 15th Street. It was a nice little church but somehow there seems a lack of the sacred reverential feeling one has in England. And it was quite a shock to see people <u>sitting down</u> all through the *Te Deum* and Creed. And we missed the prayer for the Queen and Royal Family. The President was mentioned in the prayers. A small choir of Ladies and Gentlemen sang in the organ loft, but it seemed more like a public performance than a religious service, as none or very few of the congregation joined in.

Oct 16th
I spent the morning on board writing letters. Went to town in the afternoon, and called at Balfour's office and received three home letters, one containing dear Hal's likeness. He seems to be getting so big, and tells me he has gone into <u>Bags</u>, otherwise trousers.

Oct 17th
Lunched at Mrs Menzies', afterwards we all went off on the steam yacht H M S '*Swiftsure*' just arrived in the harbour from British Columbia. The Captain received us at the gangway and most politely shewed us everything of interest.

How different the polish of an English gentleman is to the free and easy style of the Yankees. How delightful to see the 'Jacks' moving about with their open faces, weather-beaten skins, and well known blue suits with the big collars, and the nice little 'Mids' with their salute of their superior officer. There was a tame bear on board that caused a great deal of amusement, going head over heels on the deck.

We returned to Mr Daly's house for evening and night and met Captain Cross and wife, of the '[?]'.

Oct 18th
We went in the evening to see Boucicault [possibly the Irish actor Dion Boucicault] at the Opera House and enjoyed it. We have also seen *Round the World in 80 Days* taken from Jules Verne's novel. The grouping and spectacle are beautiful, not much acting in it, but it was amusing to see the typical English gentleman on the stage, so calm and deliberate, and the American, so ready with his money! There was a little girl sitting next to me, eating candies. She had such a sweet little face that I asked her if she was fond of coming to the theatre, she said, 'Oh, I'm just crazed on the theatres'. She also told me she was five, but from her remarks might have been twenty-five.

Oct 19th
Reading in the paper that there was to be a practice of a lifeboat crew, Harry and I went into town after he had finished business and lunched at the Royal. Then to a Geary Street cable car from which we changed into a steam car, which took us to the terminus of the line. The distance from San Francisco to Cliff House is about seven miles. As we had still about three to go, we were glad to find several 'stages' awaiting the passengers, fare 15 cents, everyone bundled in, and the two horses clattered off. We raised clouds of dust, and the scenery was not pretty but very bare, being mostly sand hills, but in the distance we could see Lone

Mountain with the large cross on the top, and round it all the cemeteries are grouped. Further on to our left we could see the Chinese cemeteries, or rather one large one divided by white railings into squares, each belonging to large merchants. We soon descended a steep hill or grade, and suddenly came across a view of the ocean spreading away. Half way down the hill stands Cliff House, the celebrated hotel where all the visitors go to watch the seals on the rocks, so we left the carriage and walking through the hotel grounds found ourselves on a wide balcony overhanging steep cliffs, and several hundred yards distant two conical shaped rocks sticking up out of the water, literally <u>covered with seals</u>, great fat lazy looking things, some going flop down into the sea, others creeping leisurely up the smooth steep side of the rock. They keep up a continual barking and yelping like a pack of hounds, and every one seems to feel a sort of fascination in looking at them. Double glasses are provided by the hotel and there people sit and gaze. However, we had made up our minds to go down to the beach. There were a great number of buggies and spider waggons.[4] The sun was very hot, and we found it very tiring walking about on the loose sand. The first part of the performance was an exhibition of life saving apparatus, the rocket being fired over an imaginary ship in distress. Everyone seemed very much interested but the men did not contrast favourably with the weather-beaten lifeboat men in England and were not well drilled. The men themselves were young and strong, but looked ill at ease in their new uniforms, and distressed by the heat.

The next performance was to be the launch of the lifeboat, which at that time was in the boat house high on the beach, but we had to wait an immense time, quite an hour, until it was brought out, drawn on a sort of carriage by two horses, which were furiously driven by the Captain, the remainder of the crew having got to the water's edge as they could. We took up our places on a sand hill, and could see there was another delay while the men arrived one by one and got on board and at last the boat was launched.

There was a very heavy surf breaking and everyone seemed relieved when she was fairly afloat. Had a ship really been awaiting assistance I fear it would have come too late. After rowing about for a time, the boat was returning when a wave struck her, and she capsized in the surf, and the men swimming for their lives. They fortunately were all saved, but were much exhausted. But taken all together it was a disappointing exhibition.

It is a strange wild beach, miles and miles of sand, white on the water's edge, but hilly and looking blue with the small scrub and undergrowth in the distance, and mountains beyond all but not a tree to be seen of any size, or building, except the Cliff House close at hand, or prominent rocks except the ones covered with the seals, with the Pacific spreading away and away, as I read somewhere 'there is absolutely nothing between us and Japan but the seal rocks.'

Having taken some lunch we got into one of the conveyances plying for hire and were amused to hear 'chaff' being exchanged between the drivers. We returned through the Golden Gate Park by a well-made road and very soon lost sight of the ocean, having our faces towards the city with a distant view of Lone Mountain and the cemeteries around the foot.

We arrived on board in time for 5 o'clock tea. Soon after we had to dress for a Scotch entertainment for which we had tickets. It was called the Thistle Club Ball to be held at the Union Hall. The latter is a good room for dancing, with a waxed floor. But knowing few people we took our places in the gallery to look on. It was a mixed crowd, and decidedly 'rowdy' if I may use the term. Everyone seemed to be jigging about – many children were there, and allowed to stride and push each other about on the bright floor – so different from the dignity and politeness of an English ball room. Though it is more formal it is infinitely more enjoyable. I noticed it everywhere in San Francisco, the society is so <u>mixed,</u> and they pride themselves on the feeling that 'Jack's as good as his master'. Still, I noticed some inconsistencies, and while they pretend to think nothing of birth and aristocracy, they make a great deal of it if an English Baronet or Lord marries one of their countrywomen. However, to return to the ball, we were interested to watch the pipers marching around the room and the effect of the Scottish dress was very pretty in the 'Hugs' and 'Meets', especially one danced by children. But the other dances such as polkas and waltzes were quite unlike our English ideas. Too much jumping and flying about! But Mr Banks and I had an enjoyable waltz in what an American would call an <u>old-fashioned style</u>, for both the floor and the music were good.

We left early, for walking so much through the sun and sand in the morning had tired both Harry and I.

Oct 20th
This morning I stayed on board for work etc. Being Saturday, Harry would have a long afternoon so we decided to have lunch early and go to Piedmont Springs. We took the Oakland ferry. The weather was perfect and we thoroughly enjoyed sitting on deck as we crossed the harbour. Thick crowds of shipping round the wharves and the *Superb* among the best, one of those with the dear old English flag flying, it seems strange to see everywhere the 'Stars and Stripes'. We arrived at the depot, and took a train to where the car we wanted would be, at the corner of one of the principal streets. Oakland is a pretty little town, trees planted in most of the streets and all the shops have a bright holiday air as in a watering place in England. Jackson Street is devoted to large and handsome residences, occupied by people who cross by ferry to 'Frisco to their occupations – large merchants or fortunate shareholders in mines. The car took us to the outskirts of the town, past numbers of pretty houses with their gardens full of English autumn flowers in profusion.

Then along a country road and finally branched into some
fields with the stubble standing, but at a corner of the road
where the driver waited a moment for a passenger, an old
man came out of a little corner cottage. There were a few
candies and grapes for sale. He came up to us with the air of
an old friend and said, 'Does any of ye like buttermilk? I've
got some <u>real</u> fresh!' So we got out and had a large tumbler
each, of course we bought some grapes, and took our places
in the car, which was now taking us through field after field,
the stubble brushing the wheels of the car, and we sat eating
our grapes and admiring the view and the novelty of being
taken on a tram car through such a rural district. Lake Merritt
looking so lovely in the distance, winding away between the
mountains with a beautiful blue shade on the latter.

At Piedmont there are some mineral springs enclosed in
the garden of the hotel – which is a pretty house with a verandah running round. The garden was just a deep dell and we
had to do some scrambling to the springs and tasted the water,
which was very bitter. There were great numbers of trees
called Buckeyes. They were bare of leaves and formed round
bushes, from the upper branches a sort of fruit, like large
green figs. We cut one open and found it contained a beautiful bright brown nut very much like a horse chestnut – and
poisonous. After tasting the different springs, which all had
little grottos built around and were unpleasant to the taste, we
climbed back again to the hotel, and having purchased more
grapes we sat eating them on the verandah until the car started
for Oakland. The return journey was equally delightful and
we arrived on board *Superb* just in time for tea.

We are fortunate in being here at this time of year as everyone tells us how unpleasant the high wind is that sets in about
midday in the summer and such frequent fogs in the evening.

Oct 21st
We went to the Church of the Advent this morning, a neat
stone building very comfortably fitted inside with cushions

and carpets and the light mellowed by one or two stained glass windows. We were shewn into a pew at once, and truly enjoyed the opening of the old familiar service but somehow I soon felt a want of <u>something</u>: devotion, or reverence, or I don't know what. Outwardly all was the same, but there seemed no warmth in the service. The singing was done by a mixed choir of ladies and gentlemen in the gallery, and the congregation listened. The clergymen did not look as though they belonged to the church and we missed the prayer to the Queen and Royal Family, a short one for the President being substituted. Altogether I felt as though I had been looking on at some service instead of taking part in it! There are I believe several Episcopal churches, as they are called – but the majority is Roman Catholic, and a handsome RC Cathedral, also a fine Jewish synagogue. In fact San Francisco is made of so many countries and religions, that one is in a constant state of wonder! As is usual in Roman Catholic countries and religions, people go to church in the morning, and theatres, gardens and dances in the evening, it seems so strange to see plays and operas advertised for Saturdays and Sundays.

Woodward's Gardens, a sort of zoo with variety entertainment combined is the favourite Sunday recreation for the people. Hundreds also go out by the steam cars to the Seal Rocks and dine at the Cliff House, where a band plays all afternoon on the verandah. People walk about and talk and have refreshments and later in the afternoon return in lurid carriages. All the time the seals are yelping and barking, and scrambling up the rocks or sliding down into the sea, or basking in the sun.

Oct 22nd
This afternoon I called on Mrs Brigham, having left the car I had to climb up a <u>very steep</u> but short hill. The houses on the hill were very irregular, built of wood. I arrived at the top of the hill I saw the harbour lying almost at my feet.

Several ships at anchor, with the islands in the background. It seemed so strange to be standing in a rather shabby street with such a magnificent picture close at hand. All this part of the town is most extraordinary, such steep almost perpendicular streets, the side walks as they are called are planked, and the middle of the streets made with immense round stones, most unpleasant to walk or drive on, but the buggies have been equal to anything and the horses are beautifully kept. On leaving Captain Brigham's house I found the ships and islands almost obscured by fog that hung over the water in thick clouds. It comes over the coast nearly every afternoon but does not seem to extend far on land. I returned to the ship by a different line of cars which took me through Chinatown. I only wished my ride could have been double the distance, there is so much to look at, though some of the smells were not too agreeable!

In the evening we went to the Opera House to see *Round the World in Eighty Days*. It was very entertaining, being mostly a succession of tableaux describing different countries, but I was quite as much amused by a little girl of five years who sat beside me, her mother and brother were behind but she came to take advantage of a front seat that was vacant. We soon exchanged smiles, then I asked her if she liked the acting. 'Oh,' she replied, 'I'm just crazed on theatres! We always come when a gentleman gives us a free pass. Tomorrow I'll get out all the old things I can and act all this.'

After an interval she told me she was going to take part in the Xmas Pantomime as a canary. About a hundred children came to rehearsal twice a week and marched about and were drilled for two hours. I asked her if she did not find it tiring. She looked at me rather doubtfully, then said, 'Well, now I've commenced, I guess I'll have to go on!' A gentleman who had been listening to this conversation gave her a box of candies, upon which she remarked to me, 'I'm awful fond o' candies'. It was soon time for her to put on her hat, and she turned to kiss the gentleman behind, saying, 'I ain't going yet but I'll kiss yer now anyway!'

She was terribly precocious, but so pretty and bright, I felt quite sorry to part with her.[5]

Oct 23rd

I called on Mrs Menzies, who is very hospitable, quite an American in manner, free and easy and rather loud spoken in conversation, but sings very sweetly. I strolled back through the town looking at the shops which are most attractive. The style of dress here is entirely different to England. New York is the leader of American fashion and I must say I admire it very much, with two exceptions: so much fake hair, with very little attempt to delude you into the idea that it's real, and also, that all the girls (and women too) are powdered and 'got up' to a dreadful degree, but the costumes are elegant. But I fancy the custom of powdering to excess and wearing fake hair is a 'Frisco fashion.

Feeling a little tired I went into the 'Royal' restaurant for a cup of coffee, which was delicious, accompanied by a plate of little cakes, but it is an inconvenient fashion for the cups to be without handles. It is a very pleasant restaurant to sit [in] for a few minutes. The black waiters are most civil, and one can get almost anything at a very small cost: quantities of fruit, especially melons and grapes at this season, it is rather late for most of the other fruits. I paid 15 cents for my coffee and as much cake as I could eat.

I spent the evening on board and Harry tried some new songs.

Oct 25th

Our walk into town from the ship now is most singular. We are lying alongside the wharf and have to pass through clouds of coal dust as our cargo is being discharged. And then through piles and piles of timber – 'lumber' as it is called in 'Frisco – the amount of wood is most astonishing, and when one remembers that so much building is done with wood, one need not be surprised at the great number of fires that occur. Ten minutes' walk brought us to the General Post Office where I posted letters and papers, then walked to California Street to take the cars up 'Nob' Hill.

It is the most surprising ride up hill and down hill at the same uniform speed in the cable car, as the Chinaman says, we went like 'Flashee'. Arriving at the terminus we were quite outside the town on a sandy road. We scrambled over a sand hill, through some brushwood and over a railing, we found ourselves in a large Cemetery.

I had first to empty my shoes of sand, then we walked on and found it very prettily laid out in in plots, each according to the taste of the owners, flowers and headstones. Sometimes the grass was quite level, giving the appearance of a number of small gardens. Some of them had a room built of white stone in which there were likenesses and vases of flowers and inscriptions, giving them a sort of every day [feeling] like an ordinary sitting room. I did not like it!

The graves of simpler fashion were more to my taste, the tablets being of wood in the form of a little porch, small railings also of wood round the grave and nearly all of them overgrown with flowers and creepers. The names of almost every country must have been there. San Francisco is said to be the most cosmopolitan [city] in the world. Indeed, you cannot walk the length of a street without noticing many nationalities. When we took our place in the cars it was quite a new sensation to be going downhill in that rapid smooth way, and both Harry and I 'held on' for the first few minutes, as though that would do any good, but we soon got used to it and could admire the mansions of the millionaires on either side. Very handsomely built, but they looked to me 'stuck up' and with money written on them. There were no trees near, except a few eucalyptus planted in the streets. On one side, hills quite brown after the summer heat were the background. On the other side, the Golden Gate stretching away below. The ships looking beautiful at anchor, some just arrived, others ready for sea, the clear air (it was too early for the usual fog) and brilliant sunshine making a most beautiful picture. At first sight I think the Golden Gate is somewhat disappointing, at least as one enters from the sea, but looking on it from the city it is always beautiful and constantly changing. The handsome white ferries too add so much to the scene.

Oct 26th
Today we started on the expedition of our stay in California, indeed I may say of our lives for it was more wonderful and beautiful than anything we had ever seen, all the geysers and natural hot springs (Sonoma County).

Captain and Mrs Murdoch, Mrs Bale and ourselves formed the party. We met by appointment on the Oakland ferry at 8 a.m. The morning was somewhat cloudy but we hoped for the best as everything in this excursion depended on the weather. We arrived at Oakland and took our places in the cars for South Vallejo. The trains here strike one as being immense: the great engines with their dome-shaped chimney and large brass bell, which clangs away through the whole journey. The cars are saloon-shaped with reversible seats each to hold two. There is a clear passage through the train from one end to the other, up and down which the guards are constantly passing with passenger or baggage tickets. Also boys selling candies, newspapers, periodicals, peanuts. It was amusing to look on for us as foreigners, as we are called. No wonder Americans think our railway carriages are small and cramped, and dislike having to retain one seat for hours together on a long journey. Every car is provided with a lavatory, water filter and stove. The latter I would much rather have been without, as the weather was mild, but no doubt passengers passing through the snow canyons on the overland route to New York would appreciate the stoves. The disadvantage of the cars opening out from one to the other is the constant opening and shutting of the door, often <u>banged</u> by children. On the other hand there would never be the dreadful murders and robberies that one hears of in England.

Mrs Murdoch and I were much entertained looking about, indulging often in candies we had with us. Also the grapes. There were a great many Chinamen also. They look so funny with their paper shoes, wide sleeves, round smooth faces and pig tails. They took their places in the smoking carriage with immense cigars in their mouths. They talk to each other in a sort of monotone, and it sounds like '*Ga, la, oo-la-oo*'.

Everyone here seems to have the greatest contempt for a Chinaman, even the small boys on the street throw their nutshells and orange peel at them in passing. Most of the Chinese here are of a very low class, but a few are superior, and I saw one, evidently a merchant, flush up to the eyes with indignation when a boy threw some rubbish at him, and I felt indignant too!

However, I must return to the journey. In about an hour from our starting, down came the rain in the most hopeless manner, but there was nothing for it but to proceed. At South Vallejo we took the ferry across the upper part of 'Frisco harbour. The weather cleared for a few minutes, so we were able to sit on deck, and found it a pleasant change for a quarter of an hour. Then we took the cars again, which were waiting for the ferry.

I must here take an extract from the *Century*:

For some way beyond Vallejo the railway led us through bald green pastures. On the West the rough highlands of Marin shut off the ocean; in the midst, in long, straggling, gleaming arms, the bay died out among the glass. There were few trees and few enclosures; the sun shone wide over the uplands, the distant hills stood clear against the sky. But by and by these hills began to draw nearer on either hand, and first thickets and then wood began to clothe their sides, and soon we were away from all signs of the sea's neighbourhood, mounting an inland irrigated valley. A great variety of oaks stood now severally, now in a becoming grove, among the fields and vineyards. The towns were compact, in about equal proportions of bright new wooden houses and great and growing forest trees; and the chapel bell on the engine sounded most ... that Sunday afternoon.

* * * * * *

This pleasant Napa Valley is, at its north end blockaded by our mountain (St Helena). There at Calistoga the railroad ceases, and the traveller who intends going further, to the geysers or the springs on Lake County must cross the spurs of the mountain by stage. Thus Mount St Helena is not only a summit but a frontier, and, up to the time of writing, it has stayed the progress of the iron horse.

It is difficult for a European to imagine Calistoga; the whole place is of such an accidental pattern; the very name, I hear, was invented at a supper party by the man who found the springs. The railway and the highway come up the valley about parallel to one another, the street of Calistoga joins them. A wide street with bright clean low houses, here and there a horse-post, here and there bringing town folks. Other streets are marked out *** but all the life and most of the houses of Calistoga are concentrated upon that street between the railway station and the road. I never heard it called by any name but will hazard a guess that it is either 'Washington' or 'Broadway'. Here are the blacksmiths, the chemists, the general store and Song Sam Chee the Chinese laundryman, and here is one of the hotels, Cheeseborough's whence the daring Foss, a man dear to legends, starts his horses for the geysers.

We arrived at Calistoga in the midst of the rain. The celebrated Foss[6] met us at the station, and told us it was impossible to proceed to the geysers till the weather cleared, so we wended our steps to Cheeseborough's anxious for <u>dinner</u>. It is a good-sized hotel, the bedrooms were very comfortable and clean. The dining room was very large and bare, just tables and chairs on a polished floor, wooden painted walls, the windows with a vine growing around looked into a rough garden. We began dinner with 'clam chowder', a delicacy rather like oyster soup. The meats were indifferent, but the stewed fruit, fresh milk, grapes and cakes were delicious. After dinner Mrs Murdoch and I went into the general sitting room looking onto the street, while the gentlemen proceeded to the smoke room. It was all a rather cheerless prospect as the rain still lasted. There was not a book or a paper to look at, and the usual <u>stove</u> was not so cheering as an open fireplace on a wet day!

About four o'clock we heard a clattering of horses and there was the Stage <u>from</u> the geysers, and the four horses were splashed all over with mud. There was a solitary Englishman inside. It is strange how we can be recognised at a glance in this country. We watched the Stage with great interest as we hoped to take our places in it next morning. The poor horses were glad to turn into the stable after their day's work.

In the course of the afternoon the weather cleared a little so we all strolled into the general store, and for entertainment made some trifling purchases and had a chat with the storekeeper. Then we went to a candy store and bought a supply for our journey the next day. There was not much to take our attention in the street except for two boys throwing potatoes at each other, so we went back to the hotel for tea, and after some chat went early to bed, hoping for fine weather.

Oct 27th

Our first thought on waking, was wondering if the rain had ceased. We were called at 5.30 and I rushed to the window. Every appearance of a fine day and by the time we were dressed the sun was shining brightly. Breakfast at 7 o'clock, having a few minutes before starting we went into the garden, the sun was so hot that a vapour was rising from the balcony and woodwork. The garden looked so primitive, with large piles of lumber (wood) at one side, out houses with wagons etc., and vines creeping everywhere.

Very soon the Stage came clattering up to the door and we took our places. The air was delicious, and as we rattled along the mud flew away in showers. I felt rather nervous wondering what sort of drive was before us, as everyone without exception had spoken of the danger of the road, so I think we were all relieved to find that for about an hour we drove through pleasant open country with occasional ranches, vineyards and orchards, the road gently ascending until we reached Fossville, where we again saw the celebrated Foss, a short description of him I take out of the *Century*:

> California boasts her famous stage drivers, and among the famous, Foss is not forgotten. Along the unfenced abominable mountain roads, he launches his team with small regard to human life, or the doctrine of probabilities. Flinching travellers who behold themselves coasting eternity at every corner, look with natural admiration at their driver's huge impassive fleshy countenance. Wonderful tales are current of his readiness and skill. One in particular, of how one of his horses fell at a ticklish passage of the road, and how Foss let slip the reins, and driving over the fallen animal, arrived at the next stage with only three.

Fossville is a very pretty low long house painted white with green shutters, and standing back a little from the road, well shaded by trees. We got down and walked into the house.

A magnificent fire was burning in the open grate, which we enjoyed the sight of, as the early morning had been a little chilly. There was a wide verandah running round the back of the house, and a garden. We only stayed about a quarter of an hour while the gentlemen had a cigar and a chat with Colonel Foss. Then we resumed our seats and started, not with Foss for our driver, but it was understood that his son would meet us on the way. Our driver was very civil and chatty. We seemed to be taking our time, which I thought was on account of the bad state of the road, and we were ascending all the time round the mountains. Here and there we came to parts of the road that made us give a sigh of relief when well past. Steep down thirty or forty feet on one side, and the heavy rain had broken away the edge and there seemed to be only just room for the wheels of the stage. Unfortunately the rain began again and the view was entirely hidden. Then the depth beside us got deeper and deeper and it was a most unpleasant feeling driving round sharp angles with only just the tops of the trees visible through the mist. It seemed like being suspended in mid-air. I for one heartily wished myself at the end of the journey.

All at once we heard a faint shout in the distance, which our driver returned, then explained to us that we should soon see 'Charlie' as he was bringing the stage from the geysers. Just here the weather cleared for a time and the sun came out. We could see the road going round the side of the mountain then it was lost for a time then we could trace it again, further off, and then all at once came the stage with four horses galloping. I could not imagine how we should pass each other but the two stages slackened speed. Charlie somehow managed to bring his on the sloping grass, which was not very steep just there, and jumped down. Our driver also got down. We wished him good-bye and Charlie was now our charioteer! He was about six feet tall, very quiet at first and we looked at him with some curiosity as he deliberately settled himself with the leather apron over his knees, the reins in his hands, also a whip – without a lash but like our riding whips. Almost as though they were electrified the horses started, and for the rest of the journey we seemed to fly – up hill, down hill, round corners. We (or perhaps I should say I) glanced at the precipice beside us, and held my breath while they passed what they called a 'ticklish' bit of road, but we whirled over it and were nearly at another before I had time to realise it. Once or twice we stopped, as Charlie heard us admire Chokeberries, very like the Mountain Ash. And once at a lovely clear stream that was running down the mountainside and across the road, for the horses to drink. We all had a drink also and it was deliciously cold. All about the edge pretty little ferns were growing, looking so cool and fresh.

We began to realise that the horses were as well-trained as we had heard, they seemed to understand Charlie by a word, and sometimes even without that. Once he said, addressing one of them, 'Now, Bill, what have I done to offend you? Get up!', 'Come, Ben, don't I feed yer well and look after yer well?'

Shall I ever forget that wonderful drive, the wonderful scenery around us to admire, the unusual sort of conveyance, sense of danger, beautiful trees. The quaint dry humour of our driver. He told us the names of many trees, the Madrona Manzanita, buckeye and maple. Also the hive-oak, which if touched by some people brings out a rash or irritation on their skin. We also saw a few crested quail running like partridges and here and there a squirrel.

I must not forget to mention Pine Flats, a sort of halfway house, or cottage with two good-sized rooms. In the front room, which we stepped into almost from the stage, there were some curios for sale by a nice old-fashioned couple, man and wife. Pinecones, petrifactions, walking sticks, studs, vases etc. made of Californian wood. In the open fireplace a large log was burning but though it looked cheerful we had not been feeling cold, as the rain had ceased some

time ago. The people told us that Pine Flat had been, within
a year or two, a large mining town for silver, with nearly two
thousand inhabitants. It flourished for a few months then
disappeared as rapidly as it had grown. It seemed impossible,
when we looked out at the trees and mountains, to think a
town had been there so recently, but with houses built with
wood and tents, all traces soon disappear. We chatted with
the old couple for half an hour and bought some gigantic
pinecones, and then took our places on the stage and started
once more.

About half past three, when we seemed to be in the
very heart of the mountains, Charlie pointed to a mass of
white steam or smoke rising in the distance. Remembering
Australia, I at once thought it must be a bush fire, but he
explained that it was the geysers and the steam was always
like that though more visible in some weather. Another ten
minutes' drive brought us to the door of the Geyser Hotel.
We were all rather stiff and tired, and would have liked to sit
down to dinner, but the hostess took command and said we
had much better go over to the geysers at once, and dinner
should be ready on our return. We demurred, but eventually
she carried the day, so after a cup of tea with most delicious
bread and butter, she made us take off our dresses (Mrs
Murdoch and I) and put on what she called 'dusters' – linen
overcoats, pull the hoods over our heads, put 'rubbers' on
our feet (galoshes). The gentlemen turned up the bottoms of
their trousers and each was provided with a long stick. We
followed the guide, who was a nice-looking old fellow with
a white beard clad in an entire suit of oilskins and sou'wester.
He carried a little tin cup and had also a long stick for climbing. We started down a shady glen, walking single file along
the narrow path. When we came to the bottom there was a
beautiful stream, which we crossed by a rustic bridge. By
this time we had lost sight of the steam for a few minutes,
but ascending the other side we came suddenly to the foot
of the canyon where the wonderful geysers are. We walked

slowly, following the guide and soon were enveloped in steam. Not a leaf, or tree, nor blade of grass near. The soil and rock under our feet seemed saturated with sulphur, and many other minerals. Hot springs were bubbling up from the earth all around us, some boiling hot, and as the old man dipped his cup into each we had the opportunity of tasting the different flavours, which were anything but agreeable. In some places the heat was so great we were glad to move on. In one part we were told to put one ear to the ground, there was a hearty rumbling regular sound like some immense machinery at work. This is called the 'Devil's Workshop'. The 'Witches Cauldron' is a spring of ink-black water nearly boiling. The 'Devils Pulpit' is a raised point, as we stood and jumped on it, it seemed hollow and to vibrate all through. The 'Devil's Tea Kettle' is another spring at boiling point, or nearly so. Within half a yard the steam rushes out with sufficient force to turn the tin cup rapidly around when suspended on the stick. The whole air seemed full of sulphur and we were not sorry to hear we were turning our steps towards the hotel. Leaving the Canyon we were once more amongst trees, and the old guide made us taste the cold and delicious water that ran within a few yards of the boiling steaming geysers. This place was called 'The Angel's Rest' and was certainly a great contrast to His Satanic Majesty's property.

We were truly glad to get back to the hotel after such a tiring day: early rising and breakfast, hurried lunch, seven hours' drive and a long scramble up and down through steam and sulphur! The Geyser Hotel is unlike any I have ever seen: built in two storeys with verandahs running round every bedroom opening onto the verandah. The furniture was white wood and cane, very artistic, and all the papers on the walls of the new aesthetic patterns. The 'parlour' had a polished floor with handsome bearskins thrown here and there, the bears had been killed in the neighbourhood within a few years. There was a piano and a variety of rocking chairs, which is truly American. A large open grate with pine logs burning. We all dropped into rocking chairs, and somehow chatting seems very easy when one's chair is slowly swaying to and fro, and I have been told that American ladies find 'gum chewing in a rocker' very delightful but that I have never tried!

We were soon called to dinner, it was very pleasant crossing the wide verandah. The large room was laid out with a number of small tables, but as it was the end of the season we were the only visitors. Our dinner was very well served, and we were in quite a mood to enjoy it. The proprietor's wife waited on us and it seemed strange with everything around us so American to find a perfect specimen of Cockney with that peculiar clipping of her words that sounds like affectation. After dinner we strolled out on the verandah, then the gentlemen of our party invited us into the smoke room, as the only strangers there were a doctor staying in the hotel, and his niece, so we sat round the stove and heard tales of adventures of the wonderful driving of Colonel Foss and of Californian lions and bears that had been shot in the neighbourhood. The doctor amused us by telling of a night he had when out shooting in the twylight. He fell down the hillside into a bush. On recovering himself he saw two large round eyes fixed on him through the branches. After thinking over all means of defence, he thought it might be a lion, he was surprised and delighted to see a large <u>owl</u> fly away, who was the owner of the eyes.

At 9 o'clock we began to think of retiring but it was suggested we ought to go to the bathhouse first. So, though tired, we once more started down the canyon (or glen) following the guide, but this time we each had a lantern. The bathhouse was just a log hut or house, it had a vapour bath, the vapour rising out of the ground naturally, hot and cold shower bath, and plunge bath, all natural heat of the spring and very strong [smell] of sulphur. Mrs Murdoch and I returned to the hotel, leaving the gentlemen to their dip.

Oct 28th Sunday

We were called at 6 am this morning, to be ready for our return journey. I should thoroughly enjoy a week or so in this extraordinary place, but that is out of the question. Looking out of the window, there was the vapour in clouds and right and left of the canyon, the trees and grass looking so delightfully fresh after the rain. We all met in the room we had dined in for breakfast, and had our first experience of <u>mush</u>, made of crushed wheat, (a sort of porridge) eaten with rich cream and sugar. It was delicious. There were other dishes and plenty of vegetables. Breakfast over, we walked out to have a look at the stables, also a large monkey that was perched on top of a pole.

Too soon the stage clattered up to the door with four horses and young Mr Foss, Charlie, on the box. Our bundles and boxes we had collected were put in, we took our seats, waved a final adieu to the little group on the verandah, and away we dashed. The morning was perfect and we could thoroughly enjoy all the beauties of the scenery we had missed through the rain of the day before. The day was one long beauty and delight, mountains and valleys and sunshine and it soon seemed a matter of course that we should be skirting precipices, and whirling around angles! We arrived once more at Fossville, had dinner about 2.00, then on again to Calistoga. The stage took us to the cars, and we remained in them until we reached Vallejo. Then we crossed the harbour by ferry to await our train, which should have come in about ten minutes after our arrival, but to our great annoyance we had to wait nearly two hours, which was doubly tiresome after our long drive, and there was no waiting room or even a bench. Mrs Murdoch sat on a box and I on a sail. Poor little Bertie was wearied out. There was a good number of people walking up and down. At last the cars came, I believe it was the Overland train from New York. We took our places, but had to scramble for seats as there were a good many Sunday holidaymakers. Once more

we arrived at Oakland, we went on the ferry and were soon
at San Francisco. Captain and Mrs Murdoch took a coupé[7]
and returned to their ship at the Scale Street wharf. We
returned to the *Superb* only a few minutes' walk from the
ferry. We were certainly very tired and when I went into our
cabin and threw myself down on the sofa and Harry into
his arm chair, the last three days seemed like a dream, and
in talking it over we came to the conclusion that it was the
most wonderful and enjoyable excursion we had ever made.

Oct 29th
Since coming here we have heard for the first time of
'Surprise' parties, which consist in a number of people
agreeing to take the house of a mutual friend by surprise to
spend the evening, so they club together and supply refreshments, engage musicians, and regularly take possession of
the house and treat the owner as if they were a visitor. Well,
we had a hint that a surprise party was coming on board the
Superb tonight, so anxiously awaited the time when they
would probably arrive. Mr Barker had the poop 'rigged up'
very prettily with sails and flags, the Union Jack and the
Stars and Stripes side by side.

I was glad to rest all day after the long journey. We had
tea at 6 pm and were all on the 'qui vive'. About 8 when
I was in my cabin and Harry was reading in the saloon, a
band struck up on the deck, a pretty waltz time. This was
to tell us of the party. We went out at once to receive them,
and found about 30 people, most of them we knew slightly.
The ladies came into my cabin to take off their hats, the
gentlemen and musicians went on deck, we soon followed,
and dancing commenced at once. The Officers and midshipmen came in and we danced till 11 pm then supper was
announced and we went into the saloon where we found
a great 'spread'. Everything had been brought in hampers
by the visitors. It seems rather strange, but certainly led
to a great deal of fun and it must specially be so when all

are intimate friends. After supper there was more dancing, some songs, and pipes in the saloon, and everyone seemed to be enjoying themselves. The ship must have appeared strange to the surrounding ships at the wharves. The deck covered over, the many lamps and the music going on all the time. The gangway was hoisted so that no one could come on board from the wharf without the knowledge of the lookout. About 2 o'clock everyone seemed to think of going, with the exception of two or three captains who were thoroughly enjoying pipes and songs and games, and looked as though time was a matter of indifference to them. However, when the ladies had gone I was glad to go to my cabin having thoroughly enjoyed the 'surprise party'.

Oct 30th
Though we were so late getting to bed, I felt quite rested when the dressing bell rang. When I was dressed I turned to reach my watch where I had hung it before the dancing commenced. To my surprise it was not there. Thinking Harry must have moved it, I ran out to him, but he knew nothing. So having looked everywhere, I have come to the conclusion that it has been <u>stolen</u>. Our cabin was thrown open to all, the musicians, the servants, or even the sailors could have gone, though the latter would have been questioned as there was no reason for them coming aft. It is a dreadful loss to me, as it was Harry's wedding present and some of the trinkets attached were beyond replacing. So many associations I had in connection with them. We can but put the affair in the hands of the police, though I have little hope of recovering it.

Oct 31st
I feel too sad about my watch and chain to be able to think of anything else. No other a hundred times the value could ever be the same to me! We told Mrs Menzies and Mrs Smith and they promised to see the chief of police.

Nov 1st. Thursday

Harry and I went out to the Presidio barracks to see what was advertised as a Grand Military Parade. There is a good-sized common there, and about five hundred artillery and the State Guards, taken together they are in strong contrast to a similar gathering in the dear old country. These men looked as though they had come through a hard time of work and anxiety, the regular thin angular American face, piercing eyes. Small French caps, thrush-grey uniform, square-toed boots. They gave one the impression that they could and would endure anything, but had not a particle of the precision and smartness of English soldiers when on parade. All the marching was done to the rat-tat of about a dozen drummers, no pipes and it had a most peculiar effect. There was a band on the ground but it played only at long intervals.

One or two of the officers were very handsome Southern-looking men. They were on small horses with Mexican saddles, which have wooden stirrups with long leathers, which give a peculiar effect to the rider as the legs are straight down instead of bent at the knee. The Artillery looked very well as they galloped about raising clouds of dust, and as far as we could tell they went through the drill very well.

Presidio is a holiday resort, as there are what are called 'Sunday Gardens', where bands, music and variety entertainments attract great crowds. We crushed into the cars returning to town, and were lucky to get in so soon as there seemed no extra provision for the soldiers. They ran and struggled in like a party of schoolboys, there was only standing room in the cars, but those that had seats gave them up at once to the few ladies who were in the cars. I have noticed a good deal of politeness of that kind in going about town, and have had a seat offered me in a car by a Chinaman. In that case I would have preferred standing near the door. The car was crowded with Chinamen just off a steamer, in which I was told that yellow fever was reported. However I kept my seat until a turn in the street gave me an excuse for getting out. These men looked remarkable having just landed, with each a bag or sack, containing their possessions and most of them with large cotton umbrellas, their pigtails in every variety of grease and length. A few of them wore a sort of stone or china bracelet but generally the wide sleeves cover their hands. I have sometimes liked to travel with Chinamen to watch their faces: 'so child-like and bland' as Mark Twain says, but on this occasion I was truly glad to step into the street – and leave behind them the odours of Chinatown!

Nov 2nd
We have had some groups photographed on deck of officers, men and ourselves. They returned today and are excellent, so I have been busy posting some for home, also some letters for our darling boys.

In the evening we went to see *Mazeppa* at the theatre.

Nov 3rd
This is my birthday (38th), it is strange to be spending it in California. Harry and I took a walk through the town and he gave me a very pretty little handbag made of crocodile. Then having been given some tickets for a trotting match at Oakland, we crossed the bay in the ferry, then took the cars. The race was nothing, but the journey to and from the course was very pleasant as the weather was lovely.

Nov 4th
We were not in time for church this morning as we intended. Harry sat in the saloon all morning writing letters, and I took a book on deck though it was impossible to read. The view around was so beautiful, bright and sparkling water, clear sky and sunshine. The islands, with a sort of blue bloom hanging over them, then the large white ferries crossing backwards and forwards to Oakland, Alameda, San Rafael. Here and there an Italian fisherman's boat with its raking

mast and sail, and even a Chinese junk passed. A gentleman told me that the wharf where the Italian boats were was like a bit of the Mediterranean, and it certainly made a pretty picture to see the fishermen busy on their nets and boats. The men nearly all have red caps or waist scarves, and even though they may not be handsome individually they look well collectively. We dined at 1.00 and afterwards Dr and Mrs Winter (who have taken up their abode for the return voyage) and ourselves started by the cars to Cliff House where we sat on the verandah and gazed at the seals for an hour or so, and came back in time for tea on board.

Nov 5th
Spent the morning writing letters. In the evening we went to the Palace Hotel and sat in the Court to hear the band play. They were all coloured gentlemen, mostly waiters at the hotel. The music was bright and pretty but rather too noisy for my taste. The Palace Hotel is one of the icons of San Francisco, built around a courtyard. The verandahs are around each storey, and decorated with statuary forms all around each storey. Looking up from the courtyard the effect is very pretty as it is painted the purest white, and lighted by electric light. Anyone can walk in from the street to listen to the band and the numerous 'rockers' soon had occupants gently swaying to and fro and smoking and, I need not add, spitting! Fortunately the 'cuspidors' (spittoons) are numerous.

Nov 6th
The other day Captain Dodds of the *Inversnaid*[8] brought one of his friends, Captain Sennett on board to introduce him. He is an old Ship's Captain, settled in San Francisco as a stevedore. He gave us a very warm invitation to his house and finally arranged to take Mrs Murdoch and I for a drink. Mrs Sennett and he came down to the wharf at about 2 pm, so Mrs Murdoch, having lunched with me, we were ready

to take our places in the very nice buggy, which stood waiting with a beautiful pair of black horses. We soon dashed
through the town, and then onto Cliff House, drove back
through the Golden Gate Park to Captain Sennett's house,
which is on the side of a hill, of course, commanding a beautiful view of the harbour. The house is luxuriously furnished,
the dinner beautifully cooked, by a Chinese (as I afterwards
heard). The evening passed pleasantly with chat and music.
There were several other Captains there, and the Murdochs
and ourselves stayed the night. There was quite a merry
party for breakfast; the quails on toast, the cracked wheat
'mush' and thick cream were all delicious. After breakfast
we strolled into the garden, which was deliciously sweet
after some rain, the carnations, fuchsias and geraniums looking bright and fresh. Then into the stables where the horses
were fed with bread and sugar. I notice in 'Frisco that horses
are well-kept and made a great deal of, and I think look in
much better condition than in Australian towns, though it
is well known that those cannot be excelled for endurance.
We saw two buggies start with captains for their respective
ships, Harry amongst them. Mrs Murdoch, little Bertie and
I waited to start a little later, escorted by Captain Dodds,
but before starting we were much interested in looking at
some oil paintings done by Mrs Sennett's niece, Mrs Buhl.
They were sketches from Nature, and very fine. Wonderful
to say she had only recently taken lessons, so she must have
wonderful talent.

   We walked to the cars and as the rain came on when we
reached the end of the wharf, Mrs Murdoch and Bertie
hurried to the *Sierra Estrella*, and I to the *Superb*. It is most
amusing to me to see how much Californians seem to think
of a little rain, though the ladies dress most beautifully, at
the slightest sign of a shower they take an immense cotton
umbrella, such as only an old market woman in England
would use, then 'rubbers' of all sorts are displayed in the
shop windows. Certainly I was much tempted to get one

of the lightweight waterproof cloaks, but having so many things for use on the voyage it seemed unnecessary.

Nov 10th
Today was fixed for the ship to be towed up to Port Costa to be loaded with wheat. It is one step on the way home, and though I have enjoyed the time in San Francisco, we are glad to think of being homeward bound. Of course we may be detained for weeks at Port Costa, but some of the ships have been waiting for cargo, so Harry is fortunate in having a good charter. I have heard so much of 'charter' and 'freight' lately that I begin to realise the position of the Captains who are <u>waiting</u>!

The tug came alongside about 2 pm and I stood on deck watching the wharf recede, and all the piles of lumber that I had become quite used to walking among on my way into town. The one or two British ships dipped the dear old ensign to us, among so many 'stars and stripes' it is a most cheering sight. We were about four hours towing up to Port Costa, which is situated at the top of the harbour which extends into a sort of arm, in fact the mouth of the Sacramento River. The weather as usual was exquisite and as the ship was towed along it was most enjoyable to be riding through the water on a perfectly even keel, and as the harbour became narrower we were interested in looking from side to side. We met one or two large ships on their way down to the bay, having got their cargo of wheat for which we were going up. The hills were on either side, and just beginning to put on the winter green. The few showers of rain had revived the grass almost by magic, for they had all been a dull sandy brown colour when we first arrived in California and it seemed impossible to think that as much as a blade of grass could flourish, but a week after the rain there were large patches of brilliant green.

About 5.30 we passed Port Costa (as our wharf was a little higher up). It was a most extraordinary place. Three or four wooden houses on the sides of the hills at the foot of which was the railway track, the central line from New York. A large landing stage onto which the trains were taken from the monster steamer *Solano*, but the strangest thing was to be at the terminus of so much travelling accommodation, the little wooden shed where the tickets were issued for 'Frisco etc., and another little shed for the telephone by which you could send a message into the city. This was presided over by a most countrified 'cheeky' girl who also sold grapes, apples, candies etc.

About a dozen large ships from different parts of the world were moored alongside, waiting for <u>wheat</u>, and two or three saloons or drinking shops, and a barber's shop formed the town of Port Costa.

The whole place had a most 'out-of-the-world' air, and yet there were trains, steamers and telephones! However the *Superb* went slowly by under the guidance of the little tug, and a slight angle in the coast had hidden Port Costa from us, and brought into view the Nevada Wharf, our destination. This wharf had just been completed with wood and painted a dull red colour. The railway passed along the lower storey so to speak, and the upper was reserved for the stevedores at work loading the ship.

It took some little time for the ship to be made fast. One of the sailors, in jumping onto the wharf, unfortunately broke his collar bone, which however the doctor who was with us soon set.

There were a few other ships at this wharf and it was amusing to see the knots of men standing about criticising us as a fresh arrival, and also quite a different class of ship to those usually sent for a cargo of wheat. But what struck me more than anything was the serene, clear atmosphere, the people walking about on shore, the river behind us, the hills <u>everywhere</u>, pretty little Benicia with its white buildings, and two church spires on the opposite side of the river, all looked like some scene in a play!

We had tea about 6, and there being a moon it was suggested that we walk to Port Costa and the *My Noumoue*, as we had been introduced to Captain and Mrs Cross in 'Frisco. We had to walk along the line the whole way, once we were startled by the clanging bell of the engine behind us, so we stood in a row close to the hillside while the train thundered past us. Our party was Dr and Mrs Shearer, Mrs Dove, Mrs Vale, Harry and I, and it was really amusing to see us picking the best bits of the line for walking, but we became quite clever in a few days.

We found Captain and Mrs Cross on board and we had quite a merry evening. They walked part of the way back with us, and promised to spend Sunday, the next day, with us.

Nov 11th

A glorious morning, so after sitting about on deck for a time, we all strolled up the line towards *My Noumoue*, we have no alternative, we go up the line or down the line, as it is the only available road. About a quarter of a mile from Nevada Wharf we beheld a most extraordinary sight, at least it seemed so to us. About 150 Chinamen were grouped about in a little space that had been left at the edge of the railway line. They were employed as navvies and three old cars had been converted into their dwelling place, and as their employers did not require work on Sunday, the Chinamen were having a grand old time at their hair! A few were washing clothes in tubs but the majority were either having their heads shaved or long hair brushed out or performing the office for another. I suppose they take it in turns, as in 'Frisco it is quite a common thing to see them in their barber's shops with their pigtails in hand. But on this bright and beautiful Sunday morning it had a most peculiar effect to come upon them in the open country in such a large number. Those that were being shaved (all the parts of the head) sat on an old box on the ground, with a cloth around his neck and a little piece of wood held in both hands just below the chin. His obliging friend gravely shaving away and depositing the lather from time to time on the wood. Others had their long black hair being beautifully plaited and where it was not long enough, black coarse silk mixed in. Their saucer-shaped straw hats hung in rows on their house outside. A few pigs grunted contentedly in an old truck; over their heads the washed garments were hanging to dry. I could have watched them for an hour or more, everything was strange, and the grouping like some queer picture one comes on in a curiosity shop. But we strolled quietly by, as though it were a matter of course, as we had not the slightest wish to offend them, in fact it would be more agreeable not to do so!

We walked as far as the *My Noumoue*, bringing the Crosses back with us. As we passed the Chinese encampment, the hairdressing was completed and they were evidently having their dinner, but only a few were visible, with a small blue basin in one hand scooping the food whatever it was into the mouth with chopsticks in the other. This is the only time I have ever seen chopsticks used, from the glimpse I had, they looked like two pens or pencils held between the second finger and the thumb. How they manage to get the food into the mouth I cannot imagine!

We arrived on board the *Superb* about 2 pm in time for dinner. Afterwards we went on the poop, the gentlemen with their cigars. We found a good deal to chat about, all sailors. After tea we again escorted Captain and Mrs Cross back to their own ship, and so ended our first Sunday at Port Costa.

Nov 15th
Yesterday a picnic came off that we had arranged with Captain and Mrs Cross. They had two lady friends staying on board, our party consisted of Harry and me, Dr and Mrs Shearer, Mr Hills 3rd mate, and the mids who were boat crew: Mr Hurrock, Mr Carter, Mr Seaver, Mr Sims.

We had a boat from each ship and started in company about 10 am. The morning was rather foggy, but, as we had hoped, the sun came out in about an hour. Captain Cross led the way as he said Son Soun Bay would be a good place. There were three or four guns in the party, and we had great hopes of bringing home a good bag of wild duck, but though we saw hundreds of them, they would not let us get near enough. We also saw two pelicans asleep on the water. Harry fired at them but without success, as we were anxious not to get too near. About one o'clock we did not seem nearer to the rendezvous than before, so after some consultation when the boats neared each other, we decided to land where we could, which happened to be a place that had evidently been used by fishermen, as there were old nets hanging about. We got on shore, it seemed as though it would be a swamp in wet weather, tall rushes everywhere, and frogs croaking away. The servants brought the hampers and we soon settled down to a good substantial lunch. There was a good deal of fun in laying the cloth. The sun was so hot that a sort of tent was rigged up with an old boat sail for the benefit of the ladies. After lunch we collected sticks and made a fire. For tea, we wandered about while the kettle was boiling, but there was little to see or do, except gather grass and rushes. The river wound away calm and placid on almost the same level as the land we were on. The row there and back was the best part of the day, except that in nearing home again, we found a very strong tide running, and it took some heavy pulling to get us alongside the *Superb*. The *My Noumoue*'s boat was less fortunate, or not as well-handled, as she was carried past some distance, and it was hard work to bring her back against the current. However, we were all glad to be once more safe on board, for the latter part of our row we had been on the deck and a good many sprays came over us. The picnic was not altogether a success though some parts of the day were pleasant enough.

Nov 16th

This morning we went on board the *Solano*,[9] the immense ferry that brings the overland train across the harbour from Benicia to Port Costa. The Californians claim it is the largest in the world, and it is most extraordinary. There are four funnels, seven furnaces, and indeed seen from a distance it looks unlike anything we had ever seen. It can carry two trains of twenty carriages, and it must be a strange experience to any coming from New York after the seven days' railway journey, to find the train carried over the water bodily, and in about ten minutes speeding its way along the line as usual.

At the time we went on board the *Solano* was just starting to Benicia, so we went too. The latter is a pretty little town, a few nice houses and a church, a good many cottages occupied by the men employed in stowing the ships. We walked for about an hour or so, but there being no steamer or means of getting back before 5 pm when the *Solano* would be taking the train over, the gentlemen went in search of a boat, and after some difficulty found a man who had a boat at liberty. Everything in this part of the world seems to be taken so easily, and the people are so independent, that one seems quite helpless. In England under similar circumstances there would be a dozen men ready, but here, even though there is a dollar to be made, they take it quite calmly and at their own time! And we felt fortunate that a man could be found who would take us back, even for pay. At least that was my impression.

Nov 17th

No one can imagine the enormous quantities of wheat that leave this country! This Nevada Wharf has storage for 100,000 tons of wheat. There it is sewn up beautifully in small canvas bags of about 500 lbs' weight, piled up row after row as neat and clean as possible. There is all sorts of machinery for passing the wheat into different places and men wheel it on small hand trucks to a platform where it is weighed, branded and hauled onto the different ships. The wharf is a mile and a quarter long, there are water hydrants and weighing machines at short intervals. If it took fire I think there would be little hope of saving it. Fires are taken as a matter of course, so much wood is used in building and after long months of dry weather everything is fit for burning.

In walking down the line the other evening, we saw a little opening in the hills where there were a few trees and shrubs and a wooden cross. Wondering what it could be, Harry and I climbed a strong wooden railing, slipped through some mud and rushes and arrived at the cross. Evidently it marked a <u>grave</u>. The rough outline was marked by sticks, a plant or two overgrown were on the grave and the cross at the head had just the name 'Henry Hess' painted in black letters. We wondered who the poor fellow could be and how he met with his death in that out-of-the-way spot. Yet it was quiet and peaceful, and someone had buried him decently and marked his grave with the emblem of Christianity.

Dec 1st

Our time at Port Costa is drawing to a close. The ship is loaded down with her cargo of wheat and we are to be towed down to the Bay this evening or tomorrow Sunday.

I have really enjoyed staying at this strange place: ships and wheat, hills and perfect weather seem all blended in one picture in my mind and recollection. Everything is calm and peaceful, all bustle and confusion seem far away.

I must not forget the evening Captain Cross took us to call at a house built beyond Port Costa up the side of the hill. We had a two-mile walk in the moonlight along the track. Once we had to stand aside for the train to pass, which it did with the bell clanging and an enormous red light on the front of the engine. We arrived at the gate, turned into a sort of enclosure, we could hardly see if it was a garden, but there were some low hedges. After rapping at the door, we were ushered at once into the 'parlour'. It was brilliantly lit by beautiful American lamps and was full of people, but as we afterwards learned they were all members of one family. The grandmother was in an armchair chatting and joking, the mother working at the table, an uncle and niece were at the piano, the former playing extremely well on the flute accompanied by the piano. Two or three growing boys were looking over books and papers, and in the middle of the table a large bowl of brilliant red choke-berries. They were what we would call a 'homely' family in England, probably doing all or most of the work around the place, but extremely intelligent and agreeable without the slightest formality or stuffiness. We passed the time most agreeably, then rising to go, one of the young ladies said, 'Oh you must come and see Poppa and Mowma', the 'Frisco accent for Papa and Mama, so she led us through the garden to another house close at hand. We were shewn into the drawing room, which was very modern in style and <u>grander</u>, but I did not admire it half so much as the older house with the low-ceilinged room, and the beautiful berries in the bowl. Harry and I left about 10 pm after taking a glass of Californian wine and a 'cracker' (biscuit). It was a most delicious night and it seemed strange to have to pick our way along the railway track with the water splashing and rippling at one side and the shadow of the hills at the other. When nearly at the wharf we met a party of our midshipmen strolling along, pipe in mouth – which however they removed at once, raising their caps as we passed. They are all without exception nice gentlemanly fellows.

This morning I returned from a two-day stay in San Francisco bringing with me Mrs Daly and Mrs FitzGerald. They will go back to the bay with us, the weather being fine makes it an enjoyable outing.

Dec 2nd Sunday
The tug came about midday for us, we sat on deck and
anchored about 7. We would not let Mrs Fitzgerald and Mrs
Daly return for the night so they had a second experience of
a ship's cabin.

Dec 3rd
Went into town for a few final shoppings and to make one
or two calls.
 It is very unsettling being on the eve of such a long voyage.
Everyone says this may be for five months. How shall we
get through it? However, with the Dr and his wife, Mr and
Mrs Shearer, and Mr Dove who came round from Newcastle
with us, I trust we shall form a sociable little party. A long
sea voyage is a great test of character: all ones' weaknesses
and failings are soon undisguised, and the good points as
well, though no one can be seen to advantage until they have
completely lost every trace of sea sickness, if they have it at
all. Certainly some can bear the miseries better than others!

Dec 6th
Our stay in California is at an end. The ship is ready for
sea, we are all on board, everything in our cabin is secured
against rolling, all the 'shore-going' clothes put away. Harry
is once more in his brass-bound coat and cap, and all my
superfluous knick knacks and clothes packed away, only a
warm dress and jacket and cloth hat for serviceable wear at
hand. The weather is fine and the tug is to take us through
the Golden Gate this afternoon. Once outside we shall soon
leave the land and can only hope and pray for fair winds to
take us through the long weeks, and over thousands of miles
of water!

April 12th 1884
Eighteen weeks today since we started our homeward
passage! 127 days of sky and water, and indeed we have

much to be thankful for in having more than the average of fine weather. For some days after leaving 'Frisco it was too fine, that is the wind was not strong enough to clear us of the land as soon as we should have liked. However, it gave our bodies a respite from sickness. The first strong breeze was about 20th December. It lashed for some time, so on Xmas day, Mrs Shearer and I were lying on deck and had our dinner sent up. All the midshipmen dined in the saloon, there was roast goose and a good spread of all eatables except beef and green vegetables! With a plentiful supply of bottled beer.

We rounded Cape Horn on the 6th Feb 1884, in bright clear weather but very cold, but being summertime we escaped snow and hail. Diego Ramirez was visible the day before, we had a splendid view of the islands, and went spinning along very finely. About here we sighted and spoke to several ships: *City of Glasgow*, and *Glenfinnert*. The Captains of both ships we had met in 'Frisco. No one who has not experienced it can imagine the charm there is in speaking a ship at sea, especially if there is anyone on board one knows even slightly!

We have passed through the time wonderfully well. Passing twice through the tropics we could not do much in the heat except read a little, and sit in lounge chairs. One felt too enervated to work! In the cooler weather we have walked, played cards, read – and quoits nearly every day. I got up a little concert, which was held on the main deck, but a heavy squall came up in the middle and rather spoilt it. The sailors gave an excellent entertainment (minstrels).

On the 17th March, the day we crossed the Line for the second time on this passage, one riddle was 'Why is this the smartest passage ever made?' Answer: 'Because at 1 o'clock we were on the Equator and at 8 o'clock we were in Cork' (their faces!). 'Why is Captain Berridge like a man trying to swim to a buoy?' 'Because he's trying to get to Cork.' I forgot to mention we are bound for Queenstown[10] for orders, which made the riddles a good hit!

Two days ago we were all in the highest spirits at the prospect of reaching Queenstown probably tomorrow, as we had a strong fair wind and were running 200 miles a day. Yesterday to our disgust we woke up to the fact that the wind had left us, and we were almost becalmed. A slight breeze sprang up in the evening, but ahead. This morning we were in the same position and our spirits have gone down accordingly. Here we are within 300 miles of our destination, which a fair wind would take us easily in 36 hours, and yet we cannot stir, and do not know which way the wind may come. It is too provoking. We are not alone in our misfortune, for we 'spoke' to our old friend the *Glenfinnert* yesterday morning. Here we both are, tacking and doing hardly any good! Such is life at sea!

April 13th Easter Day

This is the day we all hoped to be home for, or at least within reach of news of home, ourselves more especially as it is our darling Harold's birthday. We had hardly dared hope we should be home for dear Jesse's (the 4th April) but thought we were leaving a margin for the 13th. However, here we are with a head wind, thick weather at intervals. It has been a case of putting about at 4 am, 'All Hands' and I suppose again later in the day.

How pretty the churches will look this morning with the lovely white flowers. We have been having services only once a day (in the evening) this passage. I play the hymns and have chosen 'Christ the Lord is Risen Today' and 'Eternal Father' for this evening. Mrs Shearer and I have walked about a great deal, it is all we can do, for the cabins are too dark for reading. Harry and I had a long walk after Church. Rather cloudy, but Venus was most brilliant, casting light reflections on the water. Mrs Barker saw a peculiar sort of whale this afternoon, with a white snout. A few gulls are flying around the ship.

Our run today for the last 24 hours is only 29 miles to the good, though we have come over 100 in actual distance.

April 14th

A little excitement after breakfast, by a large Cunard steamer passing us outward bound. Another was in sight on the horizon. And a little later we passed a barque, close to us, another sail in sight. The weather cold but clear, all our thoughts are: 'How soon will the wind change?'

Harry and the officers are so disgusted that we hardly dare ask a question! There has been a great deal of rat hunting the last three days. Boxer and Lucy [I think another dog] have killed over 100 since Friday. The rats are caught in traps between decks then turned loose on the main deck for the dogs to chase. Fortunately they are killed at once.

April 17th

We have had a week of disappointments! Hoping against hope for the wind to change, but no, it blows persistently from the East. By dint of tacking and putting about, we come about 20 or 30 miles a day.

April 18th

Great excitement about 9 o'clock by 'Land' being reported and at about the same time the sail of a Pilot cutter was sighted. She made straight for us, and the Pilot stepped on board about 10. The morning was beautifully bright and clear, but a biting NE wind. We all crowded around the pilot as usual and eagerly seized the few old newspapers he brought out of his pocket. The principal news was of the death of the Duke of Albany, poor fellow. It seems but the other day he was married.

April 19th

We are creeping along the coast, still the same old 'putting about' every few hours, the occasional squall, one with hail.

We are now opposite Galley Head and in the evening sighted Kinsdale Lighthouse. This has been an interesting day, if we could take our minds off <u>longing</u> to reach the port.

First we sighted the *Earl Granville*, we saw her also off the Horn. Next we saw our old friend the *Sierra Estrella* tacking like ourselves. I wonder how the Murdochs and dear little Bertie are? All we could do was exchange a dip of the Ensign, which was repeated later in the afternoon when we were much nearer. On the chance of them seeing me I stood on the stem grating and waved my handkerchief. Mr Barker, looking through his large telescope could see them waving also, and the Ensign was dipped at once, so that was our goodbye for the present as they are bound for Liverpool.

Shortly after, a small sailing boat was seen making for us. We jumped to the conclusion it must be some communication from the Agents at Queenstown. However, as she came nearer it was evident that the man sitting in the stern was neither an agent nor his clerk, more probably a butcher canvassing for orders, or a clothier's tout. Soon he departed and another little boat was seen coming. This was a few poor fishermen with codfish and crabs for sale. Our steward soon made a bargain, with the fish tied on a rope and them hauled on board, and a bottle of rum, some tea, tobacco, salt beef and biscuits were handed back in exchange! No doubt we shall enjoy the codfish as much as the mackerel we had this morning! But never did I see three such miserable specimens. Their faces were the exact type of what one sees in the Punch cartoons: small eyes, large jaws and mouths. Their pipes had no stems, the bowl being close to their mouths, and their clothes seemed to be hanging in shreds. I could not but feel sorry for them as they sat in the boat, with the piercing wind which seemed to go through and through them. But on speaking to the Pilot he said they were probably not badly off, having a bit of land, and I suppose a pig. I certainly never saw English fishermen look so poor or uncivilised in the expression of the face.

Now I leave my diary for what we believe to be our final rubber of whist of the voyage!

What will tomorrow bring? Good news from home we hope and pray.

PART 3

After Notes

6

After the diaries

So there Maud's diaries end, in mid-air. How long did it take for them to get home from Ireland? Did they find the boys well and happy? We'll never know.

Henry and Maud travelled to Australia again in 1886–1887 and that was probably their last voyage. No further records of them show up in the passenger lists at the Public Records Office of Victoria in Melbourne.

THE DEATHS OF MAUD AND HENRY

On 15 January 1891, Henry died aged 54 from diabetes, Bright's disease (a kidney condition characterised by oedema and hypertension) and erysipelas (a painful skin infection). Harold was with him when he died, as I expect Maud was too, but she is not mentioned on the death certificate. Poor Henry – what a sad and painful end for such a strong and skilled master mariner. In his will he left £499. From his photos he looks a bit overweight and therefore probably prone to Type II diabetes. Having lived on board ship since he was 15, he had had many years of stress, discomfort, bad ventilation and a poor diet, so it is hardly surprising he developed ill health.

Maud survived Henry by 16 years. The 1891 census found her residing at 2 Avenue Crescent, Acton, London as a widow of 45 living on her own means with her sons.

Harold was then 18 and employed as a clerk in chemical manufacture, while Jesse at 17 was a banking clerk. The next census in 1901 found her at age 54 living in a boarding house at 43 Gloucester Place, Marylebone, London. Miss Emily Palmer was the head of the household and proprietor of the boarding house, and of the other eight lodgers there were five widows or spinsters aged between 37 and 72, all living on their own means. There was also a lecturer at Bedford College and his wife, and a bacteriologist.

Six years later, Maud died on 11 February 1907 aged 62, of breast cancer with a secondary infection of the liver and abdominal glands alongside exhaustion, 30 years before I was born. Jesse was with her when she died, and Harold was in Aden. She was living at Rose Cottage, Tiddington, Thame, near Oxford. She left £3,404 18s 9d.

Henry was buried on 19 January 1891, three days after he had died, in the City of Westminster Cemetery, the (now) Hanwell Cemetery.[1] I'm sure it was a bitter January day for Maud. The costs were: £1 7s 16d for the burial board fee, £1 3s 6d for the rector, 12s 6d for the clerk in orders, £3 8s for ground and grants and 9s 6d for turfing.

Maud was buried in the same grave as Henry on 15 February 1907. They lie peacefully together in a leafy cemetery not far from their home in Acton, London. There is a big crucifix at the head of the grave, and on the rounded marble footstone are the words 'He bringeth them unto the haven', a quote from Psalm 107 verse 30 of the King James Version of the Bible. Apparently this was a favourite verse of mariners. Under the words a small anchor is carved. Next to their grave is the tomb of Henry's nephew Henry Sheppard Berridge (who died on 24 December 1891 aged 23) along with his father Robert Berridge, Henry's older brother (an architect and surveyor), who died on 25 December 1902 aged 66), and wife Georgiana (died 22 April 1910, age not known).

TOWARDS THE END OF THE AGE OF SAIL

Steam vessels such as the *Cuzco* were around in the 1800s (some with sail as well), and by the 1890s they could reach Australia in 40–50 days, compared with 70–100 days in a sailing ship.[2] In part, this was due the completion of the Suez Canal, which shortened the distance to the Indian Ocean by some 350 nautical miles. Despite the advantage of speed, however, there was a cost implication since sailing ships would have needed an expensive tug to take them through the canal due to the unsuitable prevailing winds. The ability of the steamships (what Rob Mundle calls 'steam kettles') to travel the Suez Canal, coupled with their increased speed and better reliability, made them a popular choice; thus the decline of the sailing ship began to gather momentum.[3]

Jefferson writes of the demise of the clipper ships in the late 1800s and early 1900s when ship owners turned towards steam and abandoned sail. He describes the clipper ships as being vessels in which beauty and function went hand in hand, meaning that the ship breakers had a difficult time in destroying those lovely ships. As a result, in some harbours the tall ships were just left to rot and disintegrate rather than being broken apart.[4]

At this time, the construction of sailing ships had all but ceased and the existing ones were not viable as a commercial enterprise, however efficiently and carefully run. Many sailing ships (probably including the *Superb*) were sold off individually to one-ship companies, to the distress of captains and crews.[5]

One person who made some kind of transition to the steam age was the first mate of the *Superb*, David Wilson Barker. He had a lifetime interest in maritime meteorology through the long passages of time he had spent at sea, and developed further interests in ornithology and photography. He left the *Superb* in 1885, became the captain of a cable-laying ship, the *Dacia*, and was responsible for setting up the West African telegraph network. After an illustrious career and contributions to many learned societies, as well as enduring World War I at sea, he was knighted in 1919 shortly before his retirement. He became the President of the Royal Meteorological Society and continued to lecture on marine meteorology and associated subjects until his death in 1941 at the age of 82.[6]

THE *SUPERB* SCRAPPED

Lubbock describes the end of the good ship *Superb* that had travelled so bravely to Australia so many times with Henry as captain and with Maud at his side. So many voyages, so many passengers to Australia to start new lives in the colony, so many who went to widen their horizons by exploring the world.

He also quotes an account from a shipping paper stating that the *Superb* went out of control of Greens, her original owners:

Under the Norwegian flag, bound to Europe with manganese ore, she was dismasted and left to her fate on 27th April 1900. The crew were brought back to England by the British barque *Seafarer*. Eleven days later the derelict was fallen in with by the British ship *Senator* bound from British Columbia to Liverpool, when in 36°N, 32°W.

Mr John Wilson, chief officer of the *Senator*, son of a Liverpool pilot, volunteered to attempt salvage of the *Superb* with the aid of five men from the *Senator*. Sails and provisions were put on board the prize, the ships parted company, and the first news of the undertaking reached England with the *Senator*. On 27th May the *Superb* was spoken by the steamer *Buceros*, struggling bravely along in 36°, 20'W, and on 14th June the Union liner *Galeka* reported her as in 38° 20'N, 12° 44'W.

She got within 70 miles of Cape Trafalgar then accepted ordinary towage services of the Spanish steamer *Julio*, to bring her for £100 to Gibraltar, where she was safely brought to anchor on 22nd June. At Gib the old *Superb* was converted into a coal hulk, and was broken up a year later.[7]

What a sad and ignominious end to the good ship *Superb*. She was the first of Greens' iron ships among all the noble Blackwall frigates and sailed faithfully to Australia and back many times, and then to America and back to England. Henry had died by 1900, so he wouldn't have known of the *Superb*'s fate, but maybe Maud heard of it. Perhaps it brought tears to her eyes to recall those many days of sail along with her dear husband Henry.

While there continued to be some tall ships around in the 20th century, the demise of the Age of Sail was now an unstoppable force, as Lubbock describes so well:

… the world will never again know the exhilaration of watching a Blackwaller under sail, bowing in stately fashion to the short Channel seas as she surges along, the sprays flying over her fo'c'sle, the wind making music in her rigging and a white bone of foam spread on each side of her cutwater.

Imagination can only carry us a little way; it cannot put the whole picture together from the few striking pieces in its possession, such as the sheen of wet wood in the sun, the creamy iridescent sparkle of the foam to leeward and the swirling wake, the lights and shades and shadows on the sails, the curved lines of standing and running rigging, the varnish of blocks and paint of spars and such bright patches of colours as the transparent green of the curling sea, the yellow glint of copper against the bow wave, the flash of gaudy bunting and the red jackets of troops dotting along the snow-white hammock nettings.

The modern eye has no knowledge of this wonder of sea life except from pictures. Nor can the modern ear vibrate with the thunder under the forefoot; the sharp fogging clap of shaking canvas; the hiss of the surges and the suck and gushing through clanging deck-ports and gurgling scuppers; the rattle of sprays, like small shot on the deck; the singing of the shrouds and the whining hum of the backstays; nor yet with all the groans and creaks and cries of the wooden ship in a seaway.

The old Blackwall frigate has followed Nelson's wooden walls into the mists of the past.[8]

The darling boys: Jesse and Harold's lives and careers

Harold (1872–1949) married Alice Harriet Lye (1870–1934) in 1896, and in turn they also had two sons: Harold Henry (1897–1978) and Basil (1902–1960), my father. Only five months after Alice's death from cardiac failure, myocarditis and asthma on 3 January 1934, Harold married Phyllis Doyle, who had been Alice's nurse and was some 32 years his junior.

Jesse (1874–1966) married Edna Adeline Dell (1872–1945), an artist, in 1896 and they had four sons, Jesse Dell (1896–1918), Evan Denys (1902–1979), Christian Gerard (1904–1997) and Wilfred Hugh (1906–1987). A whiff of scandal surrounded Jesse when he married his second wife, parishioner Diana Beck, secretly at St Peter's, Chelmsford on 24 June 1946. He was 72 and she was 38. His first wife Edna had died on 9 May 1945.

HAROLD BERRIDGE:
ACCOMPLISHED CIVIL ENGINEER

In the year following Henry's death, on 25 May 1892, Maud arranged for Harold to be apprenticed at the age of 20 for three years to Robert Kinipple and William Jaffrey, Civil Engineers of 3 Victoria Street, 'for the purpose of teaching and instructing him in the business or profession of a civil engineer for the following three years', the indenture declares. This apprenticeship cost Maud £52 10s. Despite this, and although she is mentioned as his mother in the document, its title is, 'Mr H Berridge and Another to Messrs Kinipple and Jaffrey'. As well as the signatures of Maud, Harold, Walter Kinipple and William Jaffrey, Jesse signed as a witness to the apprenticeship deeds.

Mr Walter Robert Kinipple (1832–1901) had long been associated with harbour and dock design, breakwaters and schemes for railway works in the south-east of England. His family was Danish in origin and had been connected with such works for many generations. He was concerned with very many projects in Britain, Canada, Turkey and Spain. Of particular interest are two projects: one whereby he gave advice to the Harbour Board at Poole, Dorset (where Harold was to spend many years) about improving the depth of water in the harbour; and another pertaining to a large graving dock[1] at Blackwall for Messrs Greens. Perhaps Maud and Henry had previously decided on this path for Harold and had made some connections through their long association with Greens.

Mr William Jaffrey (1854–1905), the second signature on the apprenticeship papers, was originally an assistant to Robert Kinipple, making surveys and contract drawings, and he became a partner in the firm from 1887 to 1889. He was involved in many important civil works, including Poole Harbour and extensions to the East India graving dock, and was also consulting engineer to the Aden Port Trust, where Harold too eventually spent many years.

Harold's apprenticeship led him to a distinguished career as a civil engineer. Moreover, he was mentioned in dispatches twice for his war service in the Great War, and he was honoured with a Companion Order of the Indian Empire (CIE) and an Order of the British Empire (OBE).

Harold's obituary on Wikipedia reads:[2]

Major Harold Berridge CIE OBE (1872 – 17 June 1949) was a British civil engineer and mechanical engineer.

Berridge was born in Leicester. He was educated at the City of London School and served a civil engineering pupillage between 1890 and 1893, when he was appointed resident engineer of Poole Harbour, holding the position until 1896.

In 1897 he obtained a position with John Mowlem & Co, as an engineer on the City and South London Railway. From 1898 to 1901 he worked as an agent for W. Hill & Co in Plymouth and from 1901 to 1902 as an agent for Scott & Middleton at Pallion Shipyard. In 1902 he went to the United States as assistant superintendent of the construction of the New York City approaches of the Hudson and Manhattan Railroad tunnel under the Hudson River.

In 1904, Berridge went to Aden as Chief Engineer to the Aden Port Trust. He held this post until his retirement in 1924. In 1917 he was commissioned into the part-time Indian Defence Force as a Major and Commandant of the 45th Aden Rifles and from 1918 to 1920 he served as Garrison Engineer and Deputy Assistant Director of Railways with the Aden Field Force. He was mentioned in dispatches twice and appointed Companion of the Order of the Indian Empire (CIE) and Officer of the Order of the British Empire (OBE) in the 1919 Indian War Honours. He relinquished his commission in September 1920, but was permitted to retain his rank.

Berridge retired back to England, where he worked as assistant to the administrator of Housing Development Schemes of London County Council from 1925 to 1931.

Grace's Guide has a slightly different obituary that includes some further information on his career:

HAROLD BERRIDGE, C.I.E., O.B.E., whose death occurred at Sutton, Surrey, on 17th June 1949, at the age of seventy-seven, was elected a Member of the Institution in 1914. He was also a Member of the Institution of Civil Engineers. On the completion of his general education at the City of London School in 1888, he served a short apprenticeship with Messrs. J. J. Lane, Ltd, Phoenix Engine Works, London; and for the next three years found employment in the workshop and office of Messrs. H. Wallace and Company, manufacturing chemists. After gaining further experience under Messrs. Kinipple and Jaffery, MM. Inst.C.E., he was resident engineer at Poole Harbour from 1895 to 1897. He then held various brief appointments chiefly in connection with harbour works, and later [in New York] was assistant superintendent to the contractors for the Hudson River approach tunnels. In 1904 he was appointed port engineer at Aden, and later, chief engineer to the Aden Port Trust, a position he held for twenty years.

During the war of 1914-18 he served with the Aden Field Force Royal Engineers, with the rank of major. After acting as assistant chief engineer to the Tata Power Co, of India, for whom he was engaged on the construction of the Mulshi Dam, he returned to England in 1925, and, joining the staff of the London County Council's chief engineer's department, was responsible as principal resident officer for the construction of some 10,000 houses. Since 1931 Mr Berridge had been living in retirement.[3]

JESSE BERRIDGE: PRIEST, NOVELIST, HISTORIAN AND ARCHAEOLOGIST

Jesse Berridge was born in Milverton near Leamington in 1874. When he was three his family lived in Highgate, London, latterly moving to Acton where he attended the City of London School, leaving at the age of 16.

He was first employed as a bank clerk but was dismissed in 1895 after scandalously being 'seen out' with his newly married wife, Edna Adeline, an artist. He worked for the next ten years for the Deutsch Bank. In 1901, Jesse met the poet Edward Thomas and so began a great friendship. They both wrote poetry and had many similar traits. Jesse accompanied Edward on some of his travels, until his friend was killed by a shell at Arras in 1917. A year later he suffered another severe loss when his son Dell was also killed, also near Arras.

In 1904 Jesse decided to become a priest and enrolled as an evening student at King's College London. Having been a curate, he was ordained on 27 September 1907 at St Mary's, Chelmsford⁴ and moved to St Botolph's in Colchester in 1908. In 1915, at the age of 41, he was approved as rector to Little Baddow, Essex.

Only a week before his ordination he was praised for gallantry by the presentation of an illuminated address and a purse of ten guineas for diving off the pier at Clacton and rescuing a lad who had fallen in the water.⁵

Jesse was a popular and innovative rector. He started the first parish magazine, which still continues to this date. He also introduced shared Christmas and Armistice Day services with the then Congregational Chapel.

He was a keen and skilled local historian and archaeologist, uncovering a hidden 14th-century wall painting of St Christopher, the Norman north door, stairs to the rood loft and medieval beams of the nave roof in Little Baddow church. He published five historical novels set within Essex and reflecting local history and places (*The Tudor Rose*, *Gracys Walk*, *Brother John*, *The Stronghold* and *Bettina*, all now available as e-books!), and wrote another book, *Goddess's Grove*,⁶ which appears to be unpublished. He also uncovered ancient earthworks on Heather Hills, among many other achievements.

He retired to Colchester in 1947, dying at the age of 91 on 4 February 1966. His unmarked grave lies beside St Mary's tower at Little Baddow.⁷

Out of curiosity, I purchased Jesse's book *The Tudor Rose* online, and read it as an e-book. His books were re-published for the centenary of his arrival at Little Baddow by the Little Baddow Historical Society in 2015. Although the style is naturally enough somewhat dated because it was written in 1925, it is an interesting work (probably more so if you are a Little Baddowian, since you would recognise the places about which he writes) – a historical and mystical romance full of political intrigue, set in Tudor times in Little Baddow, and based on historical events, characters and places. Much of the prose is poetic, especially the descriptions of the countryside. It surprised me that someone so steeped in Church of England doctrine was able to write of the mystical and magic, almost pagan occurrences that make up part of the book.

An entry for King's College, London University, summarises the life of Jesse and Edna's oldest son, Jesse Dell, who was awarded the Military Cross and died in 1918 from shell fire in France:

> Lieut. Jesse Dell Berridge M.C., the eldest son of Rev. Jesse and Mrs Berridge, of Little Baddow Rectory, Essex was a member of the Faculty of Science. Entering college in 1913, he withdrew in 1915, and was gazetted to the Royal Engineers. He was awarded the Military Cross for gallantry on 28th December 1917, and was killed in action on 24th May 1918, aged 21 years.
>
> Lieutenant Jesse Dell Berridge was the eldest son of the Rev. Jesse and Mrs Berridge. He was educated at Colchester Grammar School, Christ's Hospital, where he won the Gold Medal for Chemistry, and King's College, London University. He had passed his Intermediate B.Sc. when the war broke out, and he immediately joined the O.T.C. He received his commission in the 13th South Lancashire Regiment in March 1915, and was later transferred to the Royal Engineers, going to the front in July 1915 on special service. He was wounded in December 1915, and again in July 1916. He was awarded the Military Cross at the end of 1917. *The Times, 1 June 1918.*[8]

LIVING DESCENDANTS

Maud and Henry live on in their descendants. Although Jesse's sons are now dead, their offspring are still alive. Unfortunately I don't know their names or where they live, but in due course I hope to get some clues through the Little Baddow Historical Society. My side of the family (Harold's line) has lived all over the world, including India and East Africa,[9] as was relatively commonplace in Britain's colonial past. Both Basil and my uncle Harry, Harold and Alice's sons, went to Sandhurst Military Academy and received commissions in the Indian Army: Uncle Harry was in the Gallipoli campaign and Basil fought in Burma. Harry's son Anthony had one son, Ian, and he has a family in England. My brother Ted and I, Basil's offspring, were both born in India, and between us we have six children. Ted has two grandsons, both of whom live in England. I have four granddaughters and three grandsons as well as two great-granddaughters, and we live in Australia. We are all high achievers in various fields, though not in the Church.

8

Traces and reflections

THE ST KILDA COFFEE PALACE

One of my Melbourne explorations takes me to 24 Grey
Street, St Kilda, once the St Kilda Coffee Palace[1] where
Maud and Henry stayed in 1883 and perhaps on other occasions. It is now Nomads Backpackers, but it is still there,
a squarish Victorian building with the name in relief at the
front, on a busy side street. How odd to walk where they
walked.

JEWELLERY

I am immersed in the 1800s. In a Melbourne arcade, on a day
off from transcribing the diaries, I pass a small jeweller's shop
with a silver Etruscan style Victorian locket in the window.
It catches my eye, as I have one like it at home. When my
mother died I was given a handful of jewellery, about which
I knew nothing – neither where it had come from nor to
whom it had belonged. So, having spotted this similar piece,
I arrange with the salesperson to bring in a few of mine,
including the locket, for examination. Among the pieces is
an odd necklace in the form of a snake: the head has ruby
eyes and small turquoise stones as decoration. The body of
the snake goes around the neck and clips into its head, and
from the snake's mouth hangs a small wobbly gold and glass

heart. I had always assumed this piece was Indian, but the jeweller tells me it is in fact a Victorian mourning necklace, and with a loupe shows me that behind the glass of the heart there is some grizzled hair. I am sure this is Maud's necklace, and the hair is Henry's.

PHOTOS

In 2003, I travelled to England and, among other visits, I looked up my step-grandmother, Phyllis Berridge. She was Harold's second wife, some 30 years his junior, whom he married only a few months after the death of his first wife, Alice Harriet, Phyllis having nursed her predecessor in her final illness. Phyllis gave me several old family photos, many of which were a mystery to me at the time.

Back in Australia some years later when compiling my family history and putting it online, I searched the surname Timperley and came up with a relative, Richard, a descendant of WH Timperley, from Brisbane. On making contact I found he had recently died but I was put on to some other distant cousins. One of these, Audrey Murray from Melbourne, was the family historian and she had many photos of the Timperleys and of Henry and Maud. Presumably Maud had sent these photos to her brother William Henry. Audrey kindly scanned these and sent them to me.

When I found Maud's diaries online at the National Maritime Museum at Greenwich I re-looked at all these photos, only to find they were part of Maud's story, hence many of them are presented in this book, including Maud and Henry's engagement photo. Among the photos that Phyllis gave me were ones of Henry as a baby and Maud as a girl with her brothers. Another photo that was particularly touching is a portrait of Maud's dog, Boxer, taken in Melbourne in 1883, which had clearly been carried around a great deal, being crumpled and scuffed. An inscription on the back said, 'Gone faithful friend'.

Included with the photos was the indenture document describing my grandfather Harold's apprenticeship.

HOBSON'S BAY, PORT MELBOURNE
NOVEMBER 2016

I board the tram near Southern Cross Station in Melbourne, bound for Port Melbourne. I have chosen a day when I will be there at low tide.

After we have rattled along for about half an hour, the line comes to an end, down at the bay. I grab a quick take-away coffee at a cafe near the tram stop.

There are two piers in sight, the closer one modern and in concrete, the further one older and in wood. On the land side of the walkway, expensive blocks of units fill all the space and overlook Hobson's Bay. Cyclists and walkers make their various energetic ways along the footpath. I walk down to the old wooden pier. Yes, it is the Sandridge Railway Pier that Maud and Henry came into so many times with the *Superb*. I can recognise it from the photo of the *Superb* docked at Sandridge that I had earlier discovered in the State Library of Victoria archives.

The front half of the pier has been renovated and information boards are there for tourists, but extending out into the water hundreds of large wooden square-section piers form a strange forest in the lapping water. Screeching sea birds perch and wheel around on their tops. A sign tells me that the original pier had been erected hastily when the gold rush got underway to cater for all the immigrants, and in the haste unsuitable timber had been used. The pier had thus become unsafe and most of it had been removed.

On the existing deck some large square-section timbers lie on their sides to form benches. My eye is caught by some carvings: they are named for the migrant ships that came to Melbourne in the 1960s, filled with 'ten-pound Poms' such as me and my family when we migrated to Australia in 1966.[2] And yes, there is a timber carved with the name of our Italian migrant ship, the *Castel Felice*. I realise that the newer pier, just some 500m (yards) away, is where we disembarked on a hot January day, with three young kids, on our way to Hobart, Tasmania.

So Maud's and my paths have crossed again, quite unwittingly.

ROSE COTTAGE, TIDDINGTON

I take the 'Oxford Tube' from London and find my way to Oxford railway station to get the Tiddington bus. In due course I'm dropped off at the Fox and Goat, the Tiddington pub. Rose Cottage is close by. It is a Georgian-style brick cottage on a quiet street. According to an estate agent's site on the internet it recently changed hands for a high price after extensive interior renovations. No one is at home. I decide to have a look in the village church because I'm sure she would have been involved there. After a walk across two fields and avoiding the local cows, their cowpats and bulls, I find the church, but it too is closed. Perhaps there is a plaque to Maud there, but I will have to return another day.

BLACKWALL REMNANTS

A tunnel under the Thames was opened in 1897 to link the Boroughs of Tower Hamlets and Greenwich and improve traffic in the East End of London. However, by the 1930s traffic flow exceeded its capacity, so in 1967 a second tunnel was built. The old tunnel now carries northbound traffic

and the newer one carries southbound traffic. The opening
to the old tunnel is just south of the old East India Dock.

In 2017 I travel on the Docklands Light Rail to Blackwall
looking for remnants of the shipyard where the *Superb* was
built, not knowing what to expect. I find some low-rise resi-
dential buildings looking out over Blackwall Reach. They
look like a wonderful place to live, and are within easy reach
of the city. Three longboats lazily bob on the water. At first
I don't see anything old. Then my eyes become attuned and
I begin to see old pieces of machinery, especially near the
old lock gates, covered in rust and green algae. Steel pieces
with rivet after rivet; old bollards; plants growing through
an old iron machine, it's hard to know what it could have
been used for; old bolts rusted through. I think the spirit of
the shipyards remains despite all the London traffic busily
passing by, and perhaps many drivers quite unaware of the
illustrious place that in its heyday built so many fine ships
and assisted in cementing Britain's place in the world.

NOW AND THEN

Maud and Henry lived their lives in the mid-Victorian era.
Social structures were rigid then, and upper-class people
tried to live a moral life according to the strictures of their
time. As Victorians, they had faith in science and the arts,
and the Church of England was their spiritual guiding star.
On board ship, however, they had to live by the rules of
seamanship, and adapt their customs to the needs of the
ship and the vagaries of the weather. Danger was a part of
their lives. They accepted the discomfort of seaboard conditions as a necessity and also enjoyed the luxuries of living on
land when they were able. They had a sense of exploration
and discovery when they travelled, and of course they saw
England as superior while most other places, including the
colonies, were seen in a patronising light as being 'other', and

therefore somewhat naive and inferior. Yet they seem to have been people of high moral fibre with a basically kind attitude to their fellow human beings.

Maud and Henry had Queen Victoria as their guide and moral compass and had their faith to rely on; they had a sextant and astrolabe to find their direction in the Southern Ocean, but no GPS; they had candles and wood for lights and cooking, but no electricity or refrigeration; they could add and subtract the readings for the daily ship's log, but had no computers; they wrote letters with pen and ink, not emails on a keyboard, and there was no social media. Their letters took months to reach their dear ones, not milliseconds. They performed, sang and played instruments in concerts, but had no radio, television or iTunes. They used a trumpet and flags to send messages to other ships: they had no smartphones. They spent two to three months travelling from London to Melbourne, rather than 24 hours on a jetliner. Their lives in the mid-19th century were physically difficult in many ways, and were quite simple compared with the complexity of the 21st century.

In light of this, I wonder what Maud and Henry would make of our world today, and whether they would judge their time on the whole better than ours, for all their physical discomforts. From what we can gather from their physical history and from inferences gleaned from Maud's words about their travels and lives together, I suspect they would probably be more comfortable in their time, where the structures of society were clear and firm. I do wish I could meet them for a discussion!

APPENDIX I

Henry's Merchant Navy Service

HENRY'S SERVICE BEFORE GAINING HIS MASTER'S CERTIFICATE IN 1866

Ship	Left port	To	Rank	From	To	Months
Success	London	Melbourne	Midshipman (age 15)	5-1-1852	20-10-1852	9m 15d
Lochnagar	Melbourne	Fraserburgh	Ordinary Seaman	20-10-1852	4-4-1853	5m 15d Worked passage home
Owen Glendower	London		Midshipman	18-7-1853	12-5-1854	9m 24d
"	"		"	20-7-1854	13-4-1855	8m 24d
"	"		Mid & 4th mate	16-7-1855	25-5-1856	10m 9d
Northumberland	"		3rd mate	29-4-1857	26-2-1858	9m 21d
Total						4y 0m 3d
Angelsey	London		3rd mate	2-8-1858	16-3-1859	7m 14d
Clarence	"	Calcutta	2nd mate	22-6-1859	5-3-1859	8m 13d Certified 2nd mate
"	"	"	"	21-6-1860	20-4-1861	9m 21d
Total						2y 1m 26d
Clarence	"		2nd mate	25-6-1861	10-5-1862	10m 15d
"	"		2nd mate	25-6-1862	4-5-1863	10m 4d
"	"		1st mate	25-6-1863	14-5-1864	10m 19d
"	"		1st mate	18-6-1864	8-5-1865	10m 15d
"	"		1st mate	21-7-1865	3-7-1866	11m 12d
Total						2y 8m 16d

HENRY'S CERTIFICATES OF COMPETENCY

Ordinary examination 1 March 1858 (10 Millstone Lane, Leicester)
Second Mate 2 March 1858
First Mate 15 May 1861
Master's Certificate 13 July 1866
Ordinary examination 24 July 1866

HENRY'S VOYAGES TO MELBOURNE
AS MASTER MARINER

1869 *Walmer Castle* with Maud and returning via Wellington, NZ (with troops)
1872 *Highflyer*
1873 *Highflyer*
1874 *Highflyer*
1875 *Highflyer*
1876 *Highflyer*
1877 *Highflyer* (Arrived Melbourne 5 December)
1878 *Superb*
1879 *Superb*
1880 *Superb* with Maud and the boys (Harold, 8 and Jesse, 6) to Melbourne
1881 *Superb*
1882 *Superb* with Maud
1883 *Superb* with Maud and on to San Francisco
1886 *Superb* with Maud
1888 *Superb*[1] returned via Cape Town, possibly with another Captain?

APPENDIX 2

Timperleys in Australia in the 1800s and early 1900s

In 1851 Maud's older brother William Henry (1833–1909) came to Perth, Western Australia (WA) as a young man with his father, a clergyman, and his brother Frank, leaving their mother/wife Elizabeth in England. Their arrival caused something of a scandal, since the Rev Timperley was accompanied by a pregnant lady, a Mrs Pennefather – the wife of a retired army officer who later also came to Perth – and Timperley duly had to explain to the archdeacon that the baby's father was on another ship.

Frank went on to oversee a failed agricultural enterprise and just two years later, in 1853, he and his father returned to England. Here, the Reverend Timperley eventually became a chaplain in the British Legation Service, and after his wife Elizabeth's death in 1881, he remarried into money and died a fairly wealthy man.[1] Frank, meanwhile, became an inspector of police in Mauritius in about 1869, and Maud's other brother, Oughton, became a ship's captain in the Royal Navy and died in Sydney, NSW.

William Henry, however, remained in WA, where he had various agricultural jobs around York before joining the police, becoming a constable in 1856, and an inspector, acting superintendent and second-in-command of the WA

Police Force by 1870. Mollie Bentley writes of the vicissitudes of being in the WA Police Force in those times, when most of the officers were ill-educated, had extremely poor living conditions and low salaries, and lacked the facilities and expertise to work efficiently. This meant that they were often attacked in the local press.[2]

In 1858, William Henry married Rebecca Properjohn, a butcher's daughter, in Bunbury and they produced ten children. Living in Perth a few years later, he was recommended for transfer to Champion Bay near Geraldton, north of Perth. He complained of the expense of moving, saying that 'transfers had kept him in reduced circumstances'. He was supporting his wife and six children on a salary of £200 per annum, and requested a further £20 per annum.[3] This was refused and he eventually gave in and accepted the transfer.

In 1870 he was instrumental in getting police whistles accepted as the main way of calling for assistance instead of the wooden rattles that had been used till then.[4]

Having earlier written an adverse report on the Aboriginal prison on Rottnest Island off Fremantle, he was appointed as superintendent of the prison from 1885 to 1890, and his attempts at fairness and reform are well documented, in that he encouraged the prisoners to grow vegetables to improve their diets and made sure they had blankets – many had come from the northern parts of WA and were suffering (and dying) from the colder climate. Some he deemed had been wrongfully imprisoned and they were thus repatriated, while he made sure others were prosecuted. Apparently William had hypnotic powers that were brought into use if prisoners became agitated, as he was able to calm them down.[5]

In 1890 he was appointed as resident magistrate at Bunbury, and presided over most of the south-west district of WA. He was involved with the Mechanic's Institute (at the time this was the main vehicle for adult education), Freemasonry (rising to Master Mason), and the Bunbury Orchestral Society – a driving force behind Bunbury's musical education. He was made a Companion of the Imperial Service Order on his retirement in 1905 for his services to the fledgling colony.

William (WH) Timperley was also an author, publishing two books for young people: *Bush Luck: an Australian Story* was published by the Religious Tract Society in London (no publication date); and *Harry Treverton: His Tramps and Troubles told by Himself* (1888).[6] The author of the latter is cited as Lady Broome, but in the preface she states that Mr Timperley wrote the book, while she merely made some minor editing changes. Richard Timperley, his grandson, believes this book to be autobiographical;[7] WHT's house in South Perth was called *Treverton*.

On reading *Harry Treverton*, I couldn't help noticing some similarities in writing style between William and Maud, and parallels in their devotion to Christianity, their love of nature, their taste for adventure and their belief in their social position as gentleman and lady respectively. They also both consistently longed for letters from home.

APPENDIX 3

Passenger list for the *Superb* 1883 London to Melbourne

34 passengers in all, 20 First Class, 14 in steerage.

Name	Nationality	Marital status	Age	Occupation
Edward Chas Maugham	English	Single	23	Nil
Richard Magnus	Foreigner	Single	31	Merchant
Joseph Brainard Warden	English	Single	23	Nil
Frederick Henry Benison	English	Married	28	Solicitor
Louisa Jane Benison	English	Married	24	Wife
Ralph George Pochin	English	Single	22	Nil
Chas ER Godfrey	English	Single	16	Nil
Chas Lendilow	English	Single	27	Merchant
Jessie Bullions	English	Single		Nurse

CREW LIST

I could find no record of the crew list, or of seamen leaving the *Superb* in Melbourne in 1883: they must have all stayed on for the next part of the voyage. It was normal for seamen to be released if they wished; they often went on to try their fortune in the goldfields.

Maud and Henry's families

Henry's parents	Maud's parents
Robert Sheppard Berridge (1802-1851)	**William Pasties Timperley** (1807-1888)
m 1831	m (1832)
Elizabeth Howcutt (1812-1873)	Elizabeth Bradney Evans (1807-1881)
Approx 12 children including	William Henry (1833-1909)
Robert (1836-1902)	Francis (1835-1911)
Henry (1837-1891)	Oughton (1839-?)
	Maud (1845-1907)

Henry Berridge m 1869 Maud Timperley
1. Harold (1872-1949)
2. Jesse (1874-1966)

1. Harold Berridge	**2. Jesse Berridge**
m (1) 1896 Alice Harriet Lye (1870-1934)	m (1) 1896 Edna Adeline Dell (1872-1945)
m (2) 1934 Phyllis Kathleen Doyle (1904-?)	m (2) 1946 Diana Beck (1916-?)
1. Harold Henry (1897-1978)	1. Jesse Dell (1896-1918)
2. Basil (1902-1960)	2. Evan Denys (1902-1979)
	3. Christian Gerard Timperley (1904-1997)
	4. Wilfred Hugh (1906-1987)

1. Harold Henry Berridge	
m 1922 Elizabeth Abbott Rogers (dates not known)	Offspring not known
1. Anthony (dates not known)	

2. Basil Berridge
m (1) 1934 Patricia Gwendolin
        Castleman-Smith
        (1904-1942)
m (2) 1946 Joyce Evelyn Ruscoe
        (1907-1986)

1. Harold Edward William Berridge (1935-)
2. Alice Margaret (Sally) Berridge (1937-)

Notes

A NOTE TO MAUD

1 Trollope, J, page 6.

INTRODUCTION

1 Druett, page 23.
2 The *Superb* was the first of three iron ships built by Greens.
3 See Appendix I: Timperleys in Australia.
4 See Appendix II: Henry's Merchant Navy Service.
5 See chapter 1: Greens of Blackwall.
6 National Maritime Museum, Greens of Blackwall Collection.

CHAPTER ONE

1 Wills, page 2.
2 Berridge, S, 2014.
3 Wills, page 2.
4 Lubbock, pages 103–104.
5 Lubbock, pages 131–132.
6 Lubbock, page 134.
7 See Appendix II.
8 http://sunderlandships.com/view.php?ref=157068
9 NMM PAH0672
10 Gardiner, pages 53–54.
11 Lubbock, pages 282–283.

12 Lubbock, page 130.

13 Jefferson, page 11.

14 Volo and Volo, page 161.

15 Volo and Volo, page 162.

16 Deadlights were wooden or metal covers that sealed windows or portholes in stormy weather.

17 Used to provide fresh water from seawater.

18 Agreement and Account of Crew. Agreement No. 7609, 1880, kept at St John's Maritime Museum, Newfoundland.

19 Volo and Volo, page 122.

20 Russell, pages 51–52.

21 Volo and Volo, page 50.

22 Volo and Volo, page 59; also www.mat.uc.pt/~helios/Mestre/Novemboo/H61iflan.htm for more details on how these navigational tools and others were used.

23 Russell, page 11.

24 Lubbock, pages 110–112.

25 Russell, page 43.

26 Lubbock, page 120.

27 Lubbock, pages 40–44.

28 The foremast was nearest the bow, then came the main mast, then the mizzen mast was furthest aft in a three-masted ship. Note: contemporary spelling is 'mizzen', but the diaries of the time used 'mizen'.

29 Lubbock, pages 113–119.

30 Lubbock, page 241.

31 *Superb Gazette*, 1882. Kept at National Library of Australia.

32 Agreement and Account of Crew. Agreement No. 7609, 1880. Kept at St John's Maritime Museum, Newfoundland.

33 *Superb Gazette*, 1882, page 18. Kept at National Library of Australia.

34 *Superb Gazette*, 1882, page 11. Kept at National Library of Australia.

35 Russell, pages 72–73.

36 Volo and Volo, page 160.

37 Russell, page 100.

38 Volo and Volo, page 183.

CHAPTER TWO

1 Trollope A, page xxiii.
2 Trollope A, page xxiii.
3 Trollope A, page 193.
4 Volo and Volo, pages 156–157.
5 Russell, page 146.
6 Russell, page 147.
7 Volo and Volo, page 156.
8 Volo and Volo, page 159.
9 Volo and Volo, page 162.
10 Druett, page 2.
11 *Young Lady's Companion*, page 313.
12 *Young Lady's Companion*, pages 313–346.
13 www.victorianpassage.com
14 https://gypsyscarlett.wordpress.com/2010/03/29/victorian-diaries/trackback/ Accessed 16 February 2017.
15 Russell, page 1.
16 Russell, page 2.
17 Doherty, 2010.
18 Druett, 1998.
19 Diary of Thomas Miller, National Maritime Museum, London, reference JOD/180/1.
20 The Nore is a dangerous sandbank where the Thames meets the North Sea. It was marked by a lightship and became an assembly point for ships.
21 http://thamestugs.co.uk/.
22 Tiffin is a word for lunch borrowed from Hindi.
23 Duck was a lightweight white or grey fabric used for casual trousers worn at riverbanks or the seashore. The trousers were called 'ducks'.
24 A one-act vaudeville based on a French play, *Frisette*, in which an unscrupulous landlady rents the same room to two people, one of whom works by day, the other by night.
25 Presumably the conditions made it difficult to cook anything more complex, and it probably contained seawater.
26 The top part of the mast.
27 A novel of Irish life by Samuel Lover.

28 *Superb Gazettes* 24 March 1882. National Library of
    Australia.
29 *Superb Gazettes* 1882, page 23. Kept at National Library of
    Australia.
30 Letter on a journey from England to Victoria on the sailing
    ship Superb, November 1886 – January 1887 [manuscript]
    by EJ Fuller. Held in the Vaughan Evans Library, Australian
    Maritime Museum.
31 See Maud's 1883 diary for a good description of these
    ceremonies.
32 A saloon cabin at the stern of the ship.
33 Lubbock, pages 285–286.
34 Lubbock, page 284.
35 The Great Comet of 1882 became very bright in September
    of that year and was visible in the southern hemisphere. It
    was later described as a 'sungrazing' comet – one that passes
    very close to the sun.
36 The first officer, DW Barker, had a big telescope and sent
    information about the comet (Comet b) to the Royal
    Astronomical Society in London, and it was published in the
    Monthly Notices on 10 March 1882, 42(5), page 266.
37 Lubbock, page 286.
38 Lubbock, pages 286–287.
39 Lubbock, pages 197–199.
40 Lubbock, pages 198–199.

CHAPTER THREE

1 Volo and Volo, page 167.
2 These people were Henry's brother Robert, his wife
   Georgiana and their son Henry.
3 Probably Lilian Pringle.
4 A puggaree is a thin muslin scarf wound around the head or a
   hat, to keep off the sun.
5 As Maud spelled it.
6 'Speaking' is how Maud and others described contacting
   other ships: by flags or by megaphone, if they were close
   enough.

7 Inexpressibles were extremely tightly fitting men's trousers that were meant to create the image of a Greek god. They left nothing to the imagination.

8 It was the custom for Neptune's entourage to 'shave' those men who crossed the line (Equator) for the first time. It usually ended with the passenger being dunked in seawater.

9 This is unlikely!

10 I think this would have been in the Roaring Forties, south of the Cape of Good Hope.

CHAPTER FOUR

1 *Superb Gazette* National Library of Australia.

2 'Harry' is Maud's diminutive for Henry.

3 I think this would be tuberculosis.

4 An English country dance.

5 A quote from *The Rime of the Ancient Mariner* by Samuel Taylor Coleridge.

6 Minstrel-style entertainment was acceptable in Victorian times. These words are verbatim.

7 A Burlesque tragic opera written in 1810 by William Barnes Rhodes, this is a satiric drama with comic songs.

8 A form of smelling salts containing ammonium carbonate. The smell was so pungent it was supposed to assist sick people to make a quick recovery.

9 A small archipelago of sub-Antarctic islands renowned for shipwrecks.

10 At latitude 39° I think they were picking up the Roaring Forties.

11 The building remains in 2017 as a backpacker hostel.

12 An illegal occupier of Crown land beyond the prescribed limits of settlement. By the late 1800s many had founded Australia's sheep industry and had become extremely wealthy [www.britannica.com/topic/squatter].

13 The *Maitland* was a paddle steamer that plied between Newcastle and Sydney. It was wrecked with the loss of 27 lives in May 1898.

14 Petty's Hotel at 1 York Street, Sydney, near the Botanical Gardens, was a hotel of high standards and 'the appearance of a gentleman's mansion' where the wealthy stayed in Sydney.

www.powerhousemuseum.com/imageservices/2010/04/
pettys-hotel/#sthash.Y5Bg8VVs.dpuf

15 Maud's spelling.

16 The *Cuzco*, an Orient liner, was built in 1871, and was
propelled by both steam and sail.

17 Today, this area is graced by the Sydney Opera House.

18 An English actress famed for her role as Jo, a character from
Dickens' *Bleak House*.

19 The *Morpeth* (1861–1891) was an iron paddle steamer with
two funnels and two engines, designed as a passenger vessel
for the Hunter River.

20 See https://hunterlivinghistories.com/2017/03/02/
newcastle-fortifications/

21 Long poles with a hook/spike at one end.

22 This too is Maud's comment at the time, which is not acceptable today.

23 Mollymawks, a species of albatross.

24 A small boat used for coastal navigation.

25 This is part of a poem titled 'To–' by an American poet,
Nathaniel Parker Willis, in *Poems of Early and After Years*
published in 1850 by Henry C Baird in Philadelphia.

26 This fish is the only member of the genus Coryphaena.
Usually called mahi-mahi or common dolphinfish, it is a
fast-growing, surface-dwelling ray-finned fish found in
offshore temperate, tropical and subtropical waters worldwide.

27 The Farallon Islands, or Farallones, are a group of islands and
sea stacks in the Gulf of the Farallones, off the coast of San
Francisco, California, USA.

CHAPTER FIVE

1 For information on Nob Hill, see www.sanfrancisco.travel/
article/nob-hill

2 Boats that originated in the Middle East named for their
triangular lateen sails.

3 For more about Woodward's Gardens, see www.sanfrancis-
comemories.com/woodwardsgardens/features.html

4 Small, light horse-drawn waggons with big light wheels.

5 This description is somewhat confusing since she described an almost identical episode occurring on 18 October, but this is how the entry appears.

6 Foss was famous for his wild driving of stagecoaches, and much is written about him on the internet.

7 A small two-seater car.

8 'The *Inversnaid* was a full rigger of 1614 tons with a crew of 30. In October 1886, when sailing with a cargo of coal leaving Cardiff on a voyage from Odessa to Singapore she was laden to her limits and perhaps the cargo was not properly trimmed and stowed. It is likely the load shifted, causing her to list. She struck the Hen and Chickens Rocks off Lundy Island in a force 10 gale on 15/16th October. Captain Dodds had refused help from the tugs *Brilliant Star* and *Black Cock* because of the cost. Ships papers were washed up at Clovelly and it was assumed all 30 crew [and perhaps Mrs Dodds too] were lost.' Report from the court, Merchant Shipping Act 1854 to 1876 No. 3168.

9 There is an interesting history of the *Solano*, as well as many photos from the 1800s, on the website of the American Society of Civil Engineers (http://cprr.org/Museum/Solano/).

10 Since the 1920s Queenstown has been known as Cobh. It was the final port of call for the *Titanic*.

CHAPTER SIX

1 In 1853, 12 acres of land were purchased to provide a new cemetery for the parish of St George, Hanover Square, and this was consecrated in 1854. In 1883 a further 11 acres of land were purchased and the cemetery was transferred to the Metropolitan Borough of the City of Westminster. It was renamed the Hanwell cemetery in the 1990s.

2 Russell, page 4.

3 Mundle, page 322.

4 Jefferson, pages 213–214.

5 Gardiner, pages 98–99.

6 See *Pen Portraits of Presidents – David Wilson Barker RNR FRSE* by Margaret Deacon [http://onlinelibrary.wiley.com/store].

7 Lubbock, pages 287–288.
8 Lubbock, pages 294–295.

CHAPTER SEVEN

1 *Grace's Guide to British Industrial History*, www.graces-guide.co.uk
2 'Harold Berridge' Wikipedia. The Free Encyclopedia. 9 June 2017. Web. 4 Sept 2017 s https://en.wikipedia.org/wiki/Harold_Berridge т
3 www.gracesguide.co.uk
4 *Essex County Chronicle*, 27 September 1907.
5 *Cambridge Independent Press*, 23 August 1907.
6 *Essex Chronicle*, 16 October 1942.
7 With thanks to the Little Baddow Historical Society for many facts of Jesse's life.
8 www.kingscollections.org
9 Berridge, S, *Tissue*, New York, Xlibris (2014).

CHAPTER EIGHT

1 In 1883, the term 'coffee palace' was used to indicate a temperance hotel.
2 See Berridge, S, *Tissue*.

APPENDIX 2

1 Some information from Conole, Peter, *West Australian Police Officers of Renown*, WA Police History. Unpublished.
2 Bentley, Mollie, *Grandfather was a Policeman: the Western Australian Police Force 1829–1889*, Carlisle, WA, Hesperian Press (1993).
3 Ibid, page 106.
4 Ibid, page 96.

5 Thomas, JE and Stewart, Alex, *Imprisonment in Western Australia: Evolution, Theory and Practice*, Perth, University of Western Australia Press (1978), pages 138–139.
6 © the State Library of West Australia, available on digital download for limited use.
7 Timperley, Richard, *Heroes Galore*, Brisbane, CopyRight Publishing, page 139.

HENRY'S VOYAGES TO MELBOURNE
AS MASTER MARINER

1 17 June–24 September 1888 (see *Superb Gazette* in the diary of W Barringer, a Saloon passenger). Held at the National Library of Australia.

References

Anon, *The Young Lady's Book. A manual on elegant recreations, exercises and pursuits*, London, Vizetelly, Branston and Co (1832).

Berridge, Jesse, *The Tudor Rose*, originally published by Andrew Melrose Ltd in 1925, and republished by the Little Baddow Historical Society (2015).

Berridge, Sally, *Tissue*, New York, Xlibris (2015).

Broome, Lady (Ed), with Timperley, WH as author, *Harry Treverton: His Tramps and Troubles*, London, George Routledge and Sons (1889).

Doherty, Laura Ricketson, *Annie Ricketson's Journal. The remarkable voyage of the only woman aboard a whaling ship with her sea captain husband and crew. 1871–1874*, Westminster, Maryland, Heritage Books (2010).

Druett, Joan, *Hen Frigates: Passion and Peril, Nineteenth-Century Women at Sea*, New York, Touchstone: Simon and Schuster (1998).

Gardiner, Robert (Ed), *Sail's Last Century. The merchant sailing ship 1830–1930*, Edison, Conway Maritime Press (2001).

Jefferson, Sam, *Clipper Ships and the Golden Age of Sail. Races and rivalries on the nineteenth century high seas*, London, Bloomsbury (2014).

Lubbock, Basil, *The Blackwall Frigates*, Glasgow, James Brown and Son (1922).

Mundle, Rob, *Under Full Sail*, Sydney, ABC Books: Harper Collins (2016).

Pietsch, Bodies at Sea: Travelling to Australia in the Age of Sail, *Journal of Global History* 11 (2016), 209–228 [doi: 10.1017/S1740022816000061].

Russell, Roslyn, *High Seas & High Teas. Voyaging to Australia,* Canberra, National Library of Australia (2016).

Sobel, Dava and Andrewes, William, JH, *The Illustrated Longitude. The true story of a genius who solved the greatest scientific problem of his time,* New York, Walker & Company (1988).

Thomas, JE and Stewart, Alex, *Imprisonment in Western Australia: Evolution, Theory and Practice*, Perth, University of Western Australia Press (1978).

Timperley, Richard, *Heroes Galore,* Brisbane, CopyRight Publishing (1996).

Timperley, William Henry, *Bush Luck: An Australian Story*, London, the Religious Tract Society (no year given).

Trollope, Anthony, *The Last Chronicles of Barset*, London, Penguin Books (1867), reprinted by Penguin Classics (1986).

Trollope, Joanna, *Brittania's Daughters*, London, Pimlico (2006).

Volo, Dorothy Denneen and Volo, James M, *Daily Life in the Age of Sail*, Westport, Greenwood Press (2002).

Wills, Simon, *Tracing Your Merchant Navy Ancestors: A Guide for Family Historians*, Barnsley, Pen & Sword (2012).

Wills, Simon, *Tracing Your Seafaring Ancestors*, Barnsley, Pen & Sword (2016).

Index

256 INDEX